THE DAYNCOURT COMPREHENSIVE SCHOOL
LOWER SCHOOL LIBRARY

BIRDS' EGGS
and
NESTING HABITATS

Siegfried Hoeher

Translated and Adapted by
Winwood Reade

BLANDFORD PRESS
POOLE   DORSET

English text © 1974 Blandford Press Ltd.
Link House, West Street, Poole, Dorset BH15 1LL

Reprinted 1977

World copyright © 1972
Verlag J. Neumann-Neudamm KG, Melsungen

ISBN 0 7137 06091 0

Printed in Great Britain by
Fletcher & Son Ltd, Norwich
Colour plates printed in Germany

CONTENTS

INTRODUCTION

Finding one's first bird's nest is often a matter of pure chance. People who have never taken any interest in birds happen to find a nest, perhaps in their garden or some other familiar place, and their curiosity is aroused. What sort of nest is it? Which bird does it belong to? Is it possible to identify the eggs? When will they hatch? These are some of the questions which need prompt answers if the initial interest is to be maintained. It is from such small beginnings – taking a personal interest in just one nest – that people start deliberately searching for nests and often end up by becoming passionately involved in the whole subject of how birds can be helped to survive.

This book is designed to provide information from which nests, eggs and nestlings can be identified. By using the Reference Guides (pp. 25–55) it should be possible to identify likely species from the type of habitat in which a nest is found, from details about the nest site and nest construction, as well as from the appearance of the eggs or nestlings. This tentative identification can then be checked from the detailed Species List (pp. 89–188) which includes descriptions of 280 species which breed in central Europe and/or in the British Isles. The colour plates (pp. 57–88) also provide valuable reference material.

It must be emphasized that anyone using this book – or any other – to study birds during the breeding season should do so with care and a proper sense of responsibility for the future survival of the broods. This sense of responsibility goes well beyond the limits of what might be described as the legal minimum. With very few exceptions it is *illegal* to take an egg from the nest of a wild bird. The exceptions are mainly in connection with scientific work for which a permit from the Natural Environment Research Council is essential. It is therefore much simpler for the average bird-watcher to *regard the eggs of all species as protected.* Quite apart from the legal position, egg collecting is now unnecessary because the Victorians were avid collectors and comprehensive collections had been assembled before the first quarter of this century. Many of these are now in the hands of museums and other reputable bodies, with access available to people with a bona fide interest in oology.

Legislation in the British Isles protects birds in various specific ways. Anyone studying birds in the breeding season should make themselves thoroughly familiar with the provisions of the Protection of Birds Act 1954 (the principal Act) and the Protection of Birds Act 1967. These Acts protect species that are scarce, not only from egg collectors but also from virtually any kind of wilful disturbance during the breeding season. The list of scarce species, mentioned in Schedule 1 of the Acts, is amended from time to time and it is the responsibility of every bird-watcher to keep abreast with up-to-date information about the protected species. There are special penalties which may be incurred, for instance by people who even approach a nest of a rare species. Birds can be prevented from breeding successfully by thoughtless action just as effectively as by stealing eggs. Ignorance about the habits of individual species can lead a bird-watcher, however innocently, to do things which result in the nest being deserted. Some species are more susceptible to disturbance than others and care should be taken not to linger in the vicinity of the nest. Some are liable to desert at any stage, while others are particularly susceptible at the laying stage or during the early part of the incubation period. Rare species should, of course, only be observed at a distance through binoculars unless you hold a permit from the N.E.R.C.

Photographers are naturally keen to obtain good results but all too often the best pictures risk subsequent desertion of the nest. If you look closely at the illustrations used in this book, you will see that some of them – regrettably – have been taken without sufficient regard for the safety of the nest. If a nest cannot be photographed without disturbing the surrounding cover it should not be photographed at all. When you leave a nest after photographing it there should be no trace that you have been anywhere near it. Some photographers excuse themselves by saying that the nest was only a 'common' one. Nowadays it is unfortunately not always possible to be sure whether a species is common or not. A species which is still common in one area may be endangered in another. Loss of suitable habitat, particularly in some localities, is now affecting many species which were regarded as common only a few years ago. In general, the variety of habitats is shrinking at an alarming rate. The spread of built-up areas is only one of many factors affecting the survival of birds. The removal of hedgerows, clearance of scrub, drainage of marshes, modern techniques of land management – to name but a few – are all affecting the distribution of breeding species and we can no longer be sure of retaining the number and variety of birds which we have hitherto regarded as part of our natural heritage.

There are approximately 8,600 bird species in the world today and nearly 500 of these still breed in Europe. But for how much longer? To conserve them it is essential to build up a detailed picture of all the conditions necessary for the successful breeding of each individual species. It might be argued that any form of observation during the breeding season entails the risk of disturbance and consequent failure to breed. This is true, but we need a lot more information about the habits of individual species and the risks can be minimized, provided sufficient skill and care are exercised by the ob- server. Without this necessary information we have nothing on which to base our conservation policies for the future.

Amateur bird-watchers can assist professional ornithologists in collecting nesting data provided they take the trouble to learn the necessary techniques. The best way of learning these is to follow the code of conduct set out in the British Trust for Ornithology's booklet *Nest Record Scheme* (*Field Guide No. 12*), obtainable from the B.T.O., Beech Grove, Tring, Herts. Nest record cards for completion by bird-watchers are issued free to those taking part in this scheme. The B.T.O. can also give helpful advice concerning the Protection of Birds Act.

It would be foolish to pretend that bird-watchers are not keen to see rare species at close quarters. There is no better nor safer way of doing this than by seeing them in the reserves owned by the Royal Society for the Protection of Birds, whose headquarters are at The Lodge, Sandy, Beds. Members who join the Society enjoy many privileges. To pursue any hobby successfully it is essential to keep in touch with other enthusiasts. Members of the B.T.O. and the R.S.P.B. receive publications which include the latest available news about birds, including their changing status as breeding species. By joining these societies you also help to conserve birds – a purpose which everyone who has ever watched a nest, from the building stage to the successful departure of the young, will believe to be of vital importance.

HOW TO IDENTIFY NESTS, EGGS
AND NESTLINGS

Learning to identify nests, like any other technique, is a matter of knowing what to look for and interpreting what you see. A bird often announces its presence by singing or calling from the general vicinity of the nest. It is frequently heard before it is seen but the moment it comes into view it can be identified from various field characters, such as colour, conformation, typical stance and movement in flight. Recognition of the sounds it makes usually follows sight identification. When faced with an unidentified nest there appear to be fewer criteria, so people often find it easier to wait for a sight of the bird. A nest is at least a static target for observation, and quite a lot can be learnt from the actual site of the nest as well as from its construction.

Habitats and nest sites

Many species are closely linked with a certain type of habitat, such as a seashore, a freshwater lake, wooded country, open fields and so on. Other species accept a wider choice of habitat within certain limits. Species with a wide range of distribution, which nest for instance in central Europe and in the British Isles, may adapt to whatever is available in the particular locality, and therefore show some variation in the type of site in which the nest is built and also in the material used to build it. This variation, however, is relatively minor and it is no good looking for a seashore species in the middle of a wood.

On finding an unidentified nest the first thing to do is to look at the surroundings and decide how best to describe the habitat. The next feature to concentrate on is the actual site of the nest. It may be at ground level or at some height above it, it may also be in a comparatively open situation or hidden in dense cover. The nature of the cover may also be important. Some species favour tangled growth, others prefer a leafy canopy, and so on. Burrows in the ground may be excavated by the birds

9

or taken over from a fox or rabbit. Similarly, holes in trees may be excavated by the species occupying the hole or may have been originally excavated by another species. Trees provide a variety of sites and nests may be close to the trunk or built in the outer branches. Some species show a preference for conifers and others for deciduous trees. There are crevice sites, behind loose bark or in small fissures, as well as the more obvious holes in rotting wood. Buildings provide a similar variety of sites. There are open ledges, overhanging eaves, holes and crevices, church towers with access from the exterior and so on. Man-made installations of all kinds provide a variety of sites for species which tolerate proximity to human activity.

Having decided how to classify the habitat and the nest site, it is then worth turning to the Reference Guides (pp. 25–55). Birds are listed alphabetically under the appropriate habitats and, within each habitat, according to the nest site. In cases where more than one type of habitat or site is acceptable, the name of the bird appears in more than one place. Tabular information of this kind is of necessity somewhat oversimplified, and should be regarded only as a general guide. Some species tend to spread beyond their typical habitat or nest site, adapting to the available surroundings which may differ in detail although retaining some general features in common. The Turnstone, for instance, can be described as a typical coastal species, nesting on the island of Laesö in the Kattegat and northwards along the rocky coasts of Sweden and Norway. On the Varanger peninsula in the far north, however, it nests away from the coast on stony ground.

In general, birds tend to follow fairly set patterns during the breeding season. They look for a certain type of habitat and site for the nest and then build a certain type of nest. This is followed by the egg laying, the incubation period when the bird sits on the eggs, the hatching of the eggs and finally the period of feeding and caring for the young. All this can be described as instinctive behaviour, in that each species follows a set pattern. This pattern, however, may be upset by abnormal conditions or surroundings. Birds tend to build nests in uncharacteristic sites in the heart of built-up areas. Blackbirds may choose to build in old cars, in traffic-lights and even in dark cellars, instead of choosing what would appear to be more typical sites in shrubs or trees in parks and gardens. In ·

these surroundings it is possible that the choice of site is influenced by the need to avoid disturbance and predators. The success or failure to rear a brood is a complex balance of various factors.

Types of nest

The word 'nest' suggests some kind of structure built by birds for housing their eggs. With very few exceptions all birds build nests for raising a family. The exceptions include members of the Auk family, such as Razorbill and Guillemot, which lay their eggs on bare rock without any nesting material. Nests may consist of a mere scrape in the ground with no obvious sign of construction. Oystercatchers, for instance, often lay their eggs on a layer of broken mussel shells and some of the Terns' nests are shallow scrapes with bits of shell or small pebbles dotted around the eggs.

Some ground-nesting species, such as the Pipits, build simple nests out of dry bits of grass in sites which are virtually roofed by the vegetation above. The nests of several of the Warblers are also effectively protected from above by overhanging vegetation which hides the oval structure, made out of dead grass and leaves, with only a tiny entrance-hole. Similar enclosed structures, with a small entrance at one side, are built by the Wren and the Long-tailed Tit. The Goldcrest is another species which builds an almost globular nest that is suspended from the branches of a conifer. Another type of hanging nest, so skilfully constructed that it is unmistakable, is built by the Penduline Tit – a species which breeds in central Europe. The Golden Oriole, an occasional breeder in the British Isles, builds yet another type of hanging nest – more like a cradle – slung in the angle of a fork between two horizontal branches, usually in a deciduous trees.

Then there are the open-bowl types of nest, typical of members of the Thrush family, with an inner layer of earth. Even this layer of earth can help in identifying which member of the family has built the nest; if the lining is polished smooth, often looking a very pale colour, the chances are that it belongs to a Song Thrush. Nests of several families are lodged on or between firm supports but a deep cup-shaped nest incorporating several comparatively unsteady stems – as in a reed-bed – is typical of the Reed Warblers.

Nesting material protruding from a niche or hole is often a useful sign that there is a nest hidden from view, possibly belonging to one of the Treecreepers or Wagtails. Nests in holes can also have a distinctive feature: the Nuthatch, for instance, plasters the rim of the hole to reduce it to the appropriate size. A layer of moss in the hole, often several centimetres thick and mixed with animal hair or plant down, is typical of members of the Tit family. Holes leading into steep banks are characteristic of the Kingfisher and of the Sand Martin. The former's hole is solitary while the latter species nests in colonies with a number of holes close together. Other members of the Swallow and Martin family construct nests out of straw plastered with mud, but the detail of the construction varies with the species. The Swallow builds a shallow half-cup which is open right across the top; the House Martin's nest is closed across the top except for a small entrance-hole at one side.

These examples give some indication of the ways in which nests vary in shape and construction. The fact that each species builds its own kind of nest makes identification much simpler and in many cases it only remains for the identification to be confirmed when the eggs are laid.

Types of egg

The shape, size, colour and markings – if any – all provide useful clues towards final identification. Technical descriptions of shape suffer from the fact that oologists use a variety of terms which have not yet been standardized. Technical terms are useful to the amateur in so far as they draw attention to detailed differences which might otherwise be overlooked. The terms used below are based on the system adopted by Dr Wolfgang Makatsch in his book *Kein Ei gleicht dem anderen* – a title which emphasizes the fact that no two eggs are exactly alike.

There are four basic shapes which are readily distinguishable to the experienced eye: (i) round or spherical; (ii) oval or ovate; (iii) pointed ovate, that is, tapered at one end and rounded at the other; (iv) pyriform or conical – tapered at one end and flattened at the other.

With practice these basic shapes can be differentiated further into short, normal and long. Thus a completely round egg can be described as *short elliptical*; one that is rounded but slightly elongated at both ends is *elliptical*; one that is distinctly elongated at both ends is *long elliptical*. Similarly the basic oval shape can be differentiated into *short ovate, ovate and long ovate*. The basic pointed ovate shape becomes *short-pointed ovate, pointed ovate* and *long-pointed ovate*. The basic pyriform shape becomes *short pyriform, pyriform* and *long pyriform*.

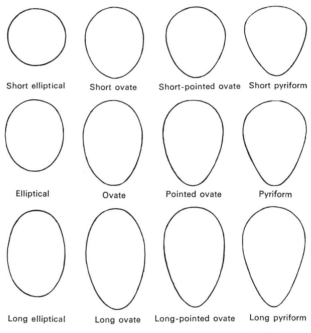

Short elliptical   Short ovate   Short-pointed ovate   Short pyriform

Elliptical   Ovate   Pointed ovate   Pyriform

Long elliptical   Long ovate   Long-pointed ovate   Long pyriform

Classification of egg shapes (based on Makatsch)

The majority of species lay eggs which are basically oval. Passerines – perching and song birds – lay eggs ovate in shape, as do Game Birds, Woodpeckers, Ducks, Geese and Gulls. Birds of Prey, such as Hobby and Peregrine, lay short ovate eggs. Cormorants are an example of long ovate. Partridges and Quail lay pointed ovate eggs; Pheasants have short-pointed ovate eggs and Dotterel eggs are long-pointed ovate. The eggs of Grebes are elliptical; Eagles and Kites are short elliptical, Swifts are long elliptical. Pyriform shaped eggs are characteristic of waders. Curlews, Godwits, Ringed Plovers and Sandpipers all lay pyriform eggs; Lapwing eggs are short pyriform, while Greenshanks, Guillemots and Razorbills lay eggs of the long pyriform shape.

The size of an egg is another diagnostic feature, although it should be remembered that measurements are averages, so that there will probably be minor differences in individual eggs in a clutch. Measurements of the length and width for each species are given in the first column of the Reference Guides (pp.48–55). Size is easily determined, but assessment of colour and marking is much more subjective. Also, there may be considerable variation in both ground colour and marking within an individual species. Some species are notoriously variable. One only has to look at a hundred or so eggs of the Guillemot to realize the amount of variation possible within one species. Similarly, a comparison of a number of eggs of the Arctic Tern and the Common Tern demonstrates the difficulty of identifying one species from another. Some of the colour plates in this book illustrate marked differences in the colour of eggs laid by one species, for example, Whitethroat (Pl. 90 and 183), Red-backed Shrike (Pl. 107, 196 and 197) and Tree Pipit (Pl. 135, 179 and 180).

The egg identification Reference Guide lists species according to their shape, in ascending order of size, and also indicates whether the eggs are white or coloured, unmarked (uniform colour) or marked (some kind of pattern of spots, blotches and so on). Further details are given in the Species List pp. 89–188.

Number of eggs in a nest

In some cases the number of eggs in a nest – assuming the bird has finished laying the clutch – can help confirm a tentative identification. For instance, many sea birds lay only one egg: Gannet, Puffin, Razorbill and Guillemot come in this category whereas Black Guillemot lays two eggs. Land birds which lay two eggs include Nightjar, Rock Dove, Honey Buzzard, Crane and Stone Curlew. Divers and Skuas also lay two eggs. Species which usually lay two eggs but occasionally three, include Swifts, Bustards and Golden Eagle. There are also species which regularly lay two to three eggs; Gulls and Terns come in this category. Species which regularly lay three eggs include Dotterel and Golden Plover. Nearly all the small Waders usually lay four eggs. Woodpecker species are mostly in the five to six category, although Black Woodpecker clutches usually have four eggs. Among the Birds of Prey Goshawk and Peregrine lay three to four eggs, Merlin four to six, Sparrowhawk three to six (frequently five) and Kestrel four to six or occasionally seven. Carrion Crows have four to seven eggs, Jays have five to seven and Magpies have six to eight. The majority of Song Birds lay five to six eggs in a clutch, sometimes more and sometimes only four. Kingfishers mostly have six in a clutch. Examples of species which have a large clutch-size are members of the Tit family which lay six to fifteen eggs and a Wryneck's nest often contains twelve eggs. Ducks, Rails and Crakes are further examples of large clutches. Ducks mostly lay seven to twelve eggs, Coot and Moorhen six to ten, Water Rail and Spotted Crake eight to fourteen. Nests with the largest number of eggs are typical of the Game Birds: Quail nine to thirteen, Pheasant eight to fifteen and Partridge with twenty-two or even twenty-seven – the latter probably due to more than one hen laying in the same nest.

In the Species List (pp. 89–188) the clutch-size is given for each species, but it should be emphasized that this figure represents the number to be expected in a 'normal' clutch. There are many outside factors, such as disturbance, which may affect the actual number laid. In addition, there are some species which are subject to considerable fluctuation in clutch-size from one year to another. One factor which may influence the number of eggs laid in a season is the amount of food available for rearing the young. Thus clutch-size is an indication of what is to be expected, rather than an unalterable number.

Arrangement of eggs as laid in a nest

The way in which eggs lie in a nest sometimes provides a clue towards the family to which they belong. For instance the eggs of Plovers, Sandpipers, Godwits, Curlew and Snipe all lie with their pointed ends towards the centre of the nest, the four eggs making the shape of a cross. Gulls' eggs, by contrast, do not look as though they had been carefully arranged, the two to three eggs suggest haphazardness and lack of pattern in the nest. Another example of an apparently tidy arrangement is seen in the nests of species of Duck. The eggs lie in a bed of soft down, suggesting concentric rings with one egg lying dead-centre. It should not be assumed, however, that birds deliberately arrange their eggs tidily or haphazardly. The way in which the eggs lie is probably due to their shape and number, as well as to the type of base on which they are laid. Almost any four eggs laid in a hollow will tend to end up with the pointed ends lying towards the centre, forming the shape of a cross. Similarly, a number of eggs laid on flat ground will tend to create an impression of careless arrangement.

Nests with eggs which are covered up

Some species cover up their eggs before leaving the nest to go and feed. If they are suddenly disturbed they will not have time to do this and the eggs are then left fully exposed to view – an easy target for any predatory species in the vicinity. If one comes across a Duck's nest without any covering of down, it is advisable to rearrange the down before leaving. Down or other material in the nest serves as camouflage for the eggs as well as reducing the loss of heat in the absence of the adult bird. Covering material may include water weeds, associated with nests of the Grebe family, and in the Tit family full clutches of eggs tend to be covered with moss, hair and other soft material in the nest. Bits of bark and wood fibres serve as a covering for Nuthatch eggs and dead leaves for the eggs of Quail.

Nests with eggs which are stained

Some species lay eggs which are chalky white, but soon become stained when lying in damp nesting material. Grebes' eggs lie in what amounts to a sodden heap of rotting vegetation. The eggs soon become rust coloured or a dirty-looking brown. This colour staining is due not only to the nature of the nesting material but also to the chemical composition of the water. On peat moors the water passing through the acid soil and humus stains eggs blackish, and water with iron-oxide constituents will stain eggs a reddish-brown. In both cases the chalky white ground colour is virtually obliterated. This is yet another example of the way in which an observer must consider habitat and site, as well as nest construction and the type of egg in the nest.

Identifying nestlings

Trying to identify a nest full of very young birds can be much more difficult than identifying a nest with eggs. The usual clues from the type of habitat, the actual site of the nest and the detail of its construction, should give some indication of the likely species. It is not always possible to get a close look at the nestlings and note the colour of the skin or down, the colour of the gape-flanges along the edge of the bill, the colour of the gape inside the mouth and possibly some tongue-spots, particularly if no trace of the inspection is to be left. It is often easier to stand some distance from the nest and wait for one of the parent birds to return to feed the young. A good look at the adults will be more informative than a furtive look at the nestlings. Above all, the survival of the brood is less likely to be endangered if the parents are not too alarmed to return with food.

In the majority of species the gape-flanges are pale yellow, others may be off-white or pinkish, and the flanges may contrast quite sharply with the colour of the gape. Inside the mouth may be pink, red, orange or yellow and there may also be tongue-spots which are whitish or blackish. Many young nestlings have bare patches of skin with only sparse down. The down may appear tufted or spiky and it may also look mottled or streaky. For instance young Skylarks have a characteristic tuft of down on the head which makes the head look as though it were slightly 'mouldy' or even diseased. A very striped appearance is typical of young Grebes, and when identifying young Rails or Crakes the colour of the bill and feet may be significant.

Some young birds are helpless when hatched, while others can move around freely within a few hours of hatching. Species which are helpless are described as *altricial* and are also said to be *nidicolous*, as they remain in the nest for some time and are fed by their parents. In these species the succession of down and development of plumage is comparatively slow and it may be several weeks before the young are ready to leave the nest. Species which are able to move about freely soon after hatching are described as *precocial* and *nidifugous*. They are well covered with down and very mobile, being able to fend for themselves to a considerable extent although they remain in the vicinity of the nest or place where they hatched for some days.

Behaviour of parents and young

The first outburst of song, heard early in the year, is an indication that for many species the breeding season has started. Song is linked with the reproductive cycle and often accompanies various courtship displays which lead to mating. Nest building and egg laying are followed by the incubation period which ends with hatching. The roles played by the males and females in nest building and incubating vary with the species. In many of the passerines incubation is carried out only by the females. In the Ducks and Geese, the females often incubate while the males stand guard in the vicinity of the nest. Species in which the males share in the duties of incubation include Guillemot, Razorbill, Avocet, Terns, Plovers and Pigeons. In many cases when the young have hatched the eggshells are dropped over the side of the nest or carried away by the parent bird; in others, bits of shell are left lying in the nest or are eaten.

Feeding behaviour also varies according to the species. Many young passerines are fed by the parent placing food directly into the gape of the nestling. Not all young birds, however, await the delivery of food with open mouths. Young Owls, for instance, are virtually blind and have to be encouraged to take food; the parent does this by touching the nestlings' bills with bits of food. Young Pigeons, for the first few days of their lives, thrust their bills into the side of the parent's bill and take 'pigeon's milk', a substance produced in the adult's crop. Young Cormorants feed on partly digested food taken from the throat-pouch of the parent. Gulls regurgitate, holding the food until the young take it directly from the adult's bill. Ducks and Game Birds are different again, as the young can accompany the adults on food forays shortly after hatching.

Parental care includes nest sanitation – the removal of excrement from the nest – as well as keeping the young warm or shading them from excessive heat. Guarding the nest, whether it contains eggs or young, is another aspect of parental behaviour which varies with the species and the respective roles of male and female are well worth observing. The reactions of young to warning calls or signals from the parents, and the action taken by the parents when predators are in the vicinity, all vary according to the species. Behaviour of this kind is characteristic of the species and, to an experienced observer, it may even indicate where the nest is situated.

Young Bitterns react to the parent's warning call by adopting a concealment posture, also typical of the adults. They stretch the neck and bill to a vertical line and remain perfectly still looking like dead sticks or reed stems. Distracting the attention of a predator away from the nest or from young near the nest is another form of protective behaviour. Parent Lapwings, for example, act as though injured, fluttering helplessly along the ground as if barely able to fly, gradually leading the predator away from the nest or young. Other species adopt more aggressive measures. Skuas, for instance, may fly directly at an intruder, calling loudly and harassing the person with a well-aimed dive-bombing technique. Terns also fly around, 'scolding' and making diving attacks. Any suggestion of an aggressive attack by an Owl should be treated seriously as people have suffered severe injuries when investigating nests. In the event of any hint of such behaviour the human intruder should move right away from the vicinity of the nest.

Nesting dates and number of broods

The calendar months in which individual species nest can be stated with reasonable accuracy. Actual dates may vary within a week or two according to temperature and weather conditions. Also, species which have a wide breeding distribution may vary by about a month according to the latitude of the different parts of their range. The Reference Guide (pp. 25–47) gives the calendar months during which nests with eggs are likely to be found for each species.

The success or failure of a brood is affected by various factors. It is obviously essential that there should be enough of the right sort of food available at the time when the young require a steady supply of food. For instance, the Tit family rear their first broods from late April when insects are likely to be plentiful. Species such as Crossbill, which feed on ripe conifer seeds, are able to start their breeding season much earlier. In central Europe some nests have young in them in any month of the year, with the possible exception of the period between July and November. Nests of Raven, Ural Owl and White-tailed Eagle are often found by the end of February. Rooks and Carrion Crows nest in March and there may also be nests of Robin and Mistle Thrush. By the end of March

Blackbirds and Lapwings are usually hatching out eggs. April brings nests of Dunnock, Song Thrush and Magpie.

After the arrival of the spring migrants the breeding season builds up to a peak and many species nest for the first time from April to June. Late breeders on the Continent include Golden Oriole, Red-breasted Flycatcher and Scarlet Grosbeak and nests of these species are often not to be found until June. In Britain Spotted Flycatcher and Pied Flycatcher nests are found from May to June.

A number of species regularly rear only one brood, although many of them can lay a replacement clutch if the first attempt at breeding fails for any reason. On the Continent, for instance, single broods are frequently recorded for Golden Oriole, Hawfinch, Tree Pipit, Nuthatch, Nightingale, Hoopoe and Roller, as well as many of the Warblers, Owls, Woodpeckers, Ducks and Geese, Terns and Gulls. Species which run the risk of a high rate of breeding failure tend, in general, to lay large clutches.

Many migratory species rear two broods or more and it has been suggested that this compensates for losses on the long journeys to and from the breeding areas. Nevertheless, there are examples of non-migratory species, such as House Sparrow, which may rear as many as four broods in a year.

There are records of pairs of birds splitting up before one brood has been completely reared and starting another nest. In such cases the male takes over the care of the first brood while the female lays another clutch and starts incubating them, the male rejoining her to help feed the young of the second brood. Instances of this have been recorded for Robin, Kingfisher, Moorhen, Little Grebe, Pigeons, Little Bittern, Nightjar, Rock Partridges and Barn Owl. There are also instances of more than one female laying in the same nest, giving the impression to a casual observer that an exceptionally large number of eggs have been laid. The careful observer may come across nests in which an adult of one species shares in the feeding of young which belong to another species. And there is always the possibility of finding a nest with a Cuckoo in it.

Nest parasitism

Cuckoos do not build nests of their own. They leave the whole process of incubation and rearing their young to adults of other species. The latter are described as foster-parents and the Cuckoo as *nest parasitic*. Species which frequently act as foster-parents may also be described as *host specific*.

A female Cuckoo mates with several males and she may lay as many as twenty-two eggs in a season. The laying period is usually from 20th May to mid-June. The actual number of eggs laid by any one female varies considerably and is primarily regulated by the availability of nests suitable for parasitism. To the human observer the finding of sufficient nests of potential fosterers, all apparently well hidden from view, seems to present the Cuckoo with a formidable task. Observations show, however, that the female Cuckoo keeps watch on host species while they are at the nest-building stage. She nearly always waits until the first egg, or two eggs, are laid by the host before laying her own egg in the nest. She usually removes one of the host's eggs in her bill as she leaves the nest, but this procedure is not always followed. It is suggested, however, that failure to do so means she was disturbed while laying her own egg.

Cuckoos lay their own eggs at intervals of forty-eight hours and laying nearly always takes place during the afternoon. Observations confirm that a Cuckoo is able to alight at a very small nest and lay her egg safely in it, even when the nest is in a relatively unstable site. Reed Warblers, for example, are often successfully parasitized. When the host species is a hole-nester, it has been suggested by some ornithologists that the Cuckoo lays her egg on the ground and then carries it in her bill, dropping it through the entrance-hole. This procedure, however, was not confirmed by Edgar Chance who studied the Cuckoo from 1918 to 1921 and published his observations in *The Cuckoo's Secret* (Sidgwick & Jackson, 1922).

It is known that each female Cuckoo keeps watch on one particular species, which is already an established host, and tries to lay all her eggs in nests built by this species. In many cases the Cuckoo's egg bears a remarkable resemblance to that of the host. This is well illustrated in the photograph of a Marsh Warbler's nest (Pl. 85) and of a Robin's nest (Pl. 77). There is an obvious biological advantage to the Cuckoo in laying only one type of egg and it is suggested that each Cuckoo specializes in attaching herself to one host species. As a corollary, it is also suggested that the species she selects is the same one by which she was originally reared.

21

Cuckoos are also known to lay eggs which do not resemble the host's eggs and even in such cases no egg is removed from the host's nest. Another example of successful nest parasitism in which the eggs do not match those of the host species occurs in the *Icteridae* or Cow-birds of America. This suggests that egg mimicry is not essential to successful nest parasitism. The fact that the eggs of one particular Cuckoo show remarkably little variation makes it possible for an observer, working within a reasonably small area, to identify eggs which belong to one particular female.

There are about 180 different host species on record. Many of these could be described as accidental Cuckoo hosts. There are comparatively few species in which the relationship has developed so closely that the fosterers can be described as host specific. In Germany, White Wagtail and Reed Warbler are regarded as host specific; other frequent victims include Meadow Pipit, Robin, Red-backed Shrike, Wren, Marsh Warbler, Sedge Warbler, Blue-headed Wagtail, Grey Wagtail and Garden Warbler. In Britain, the probable order of frequency is Meadow Pipit, Dunnock, Reed Warbler, Pied Wagtail, Robin, Tree Pipit and Sedge Warbler.

The success or failure of a species as a host is dependent on many factors. Obviously the 'foreign' egg must be acceptable to the host but its acceptance is not necessarily determined by the extent to which it matches – or mimics – the host's own eggs. The whole question of a bird's ability to recognize individual eggs is one on which a lot more information is needed. Another factor is the degree of disturbance caused by the Cuckoo when laying its egg. Some species are particularly sensitive to disturbance. The entrance-hole to the nests of some Warblers is so narrow that the Cuckoo can scarcely avoid damaging the structure, and when this happens the Warblers nearly always desert the nest. The Wren, on the other hand, which has a similar small entrance-hole, is apparently less likely to desert.

The abundance of Cuckoos in some areas indicates the survival value of this form of parasitism. The disadvantage to the host species, however, is very marked since no brood of its own is reared with a Cuckoo in its nest.

NEST RECORD CARD

BRITISH TRUST FOR ORNITHOLOGY, BEECH GROVE, TRING, HERTS.

Please consult instruction leaflet for method of completing cards, advice on visiting nests, and what observations are most useful.

A few reminders:-
1. Clubs and schools should give their name as well as the observer's.
2. Use one card for each nesting attempt, even if a nest is used twice.
3. Record all counts of eggs or young, even if number is unchanged.
4. To avoid mistakes, please write the month, e.g. 5 April, not 5/4.
5. Accurate counts of eggs and young are important, but if there is uncertainty put a ✓, or put brackets round the probable number.
6. Do not forget to record any eggs remaining unhatched.
7. Final visit: please enter date and nest-contents overleaf, and indicate your findings under "Outcome of Nest" below. The central space below can be used for further visits and/or notes.

RECORD ONLY WHAT YOU OBSERVE: PLEASE MAKE NO GUESSES

4   APR   1400   2 young being fed by parent and another young heard calling in bushes nearby.

See card no. 16 for second brood of this pair.

OUTCOME OF NEST

If you have positive evidence that the young left safely, or of failure, please put a cross (☒) in the appropriate box or boxes below. Otherwise mark the appropriate "Outcome Unknown" box.

OUTCOME UNKNOWN
- Because evidence for or against success is inconclusive ☐
- Because observations on nest were not continued ☐

EVIDENCE FOR SUCCESS
- Young capable of leaving nest when last seen ☐
- Young: seen leaving naturally ☐ left when approached ☐
- Young seen and/or heard near nest ☒
- Parent bird(s): giving alarm calls ☐ carrying food ☐
- In nest: hatched shells ☐ feather scale ☐ droppings ☐
- Any other evidence:-

EVIDENCE FOR FAILURE
- Nest: empty ☐ damaged ☐ fallen ☐ flooded ☐ removed ☐
- Eggs: damaged ☐ deserted ☐ all infertile or addled ☐
- Young: all dead, uninjured ☐ all dead, 1 or more injured ☐
- Any other evidence (e.g. type of weather causing failure, species of predator if seen, etc.):-

| OBSERVER | | | | | SPECIES | SONG THRUSH. (16) | YEAR 19 72 | B.T.O Ref. |

OBSERVER R.A. MORGAN.

SPECIES SONG THRUSH. (16)

YEAR 19 72

DATE Day : Month	G.M.T.	EGGS	YNG.	NO. of EGGS or YOUNG at each visit. Record here stage of building; if bird sitting; if eggs warm; age of young; ring nos. etc.
11 FEB	0930			Started Building.
15 FEB	1430			Basic Platform Finished.
27 FEB	1630			Lining Completed.
4 MAR	1600	3		Cold.
6 MAR				Sitting all day.
7 MAR	1400	4		Warm.
14 MAR				Sitting adult.
15 MAR	1100	4		Warm.
22 MAR	1300		4	Eyes closed, almost naked : ca 2 days old
28 MAR	1100		4	Young Ringed CV07169-72
1 APR	1230		2	1 young seen leaving nest.

COUNTY HERTS.

LOCALITY (place-name) BEECH GROVE TRING   Grid Ref SP932118.

ALTITUDE above sea level 445 ft.

HABITAT Delete those inapplicable:- RURAL/SUBURBAN/URBAN

Mature Garden bordering large house.

NEST SITE 45' tall Cypress tree among shrubs at garden edge. In lower hanging branches.

Height above ground or cliff-base 8 ft.

Further visits, notes on outcome, etc. – ON BACK

Office Use Only

D

C

H

F

If this record is entered on ATLAS CARD put X in box.

24

GUIDE TO NEST IDENTIFICATION

Species are listed alphabetically under habitats and sites. Data are based largely on observations recorded in central Europe. The majority of species also breed in the British Isles and these are marked with an asterisk (*). In general, the habits of a species are much the same throughout the breeding range, although dates of nesting may vary at different latitudes and altitudes. The last column indicates the months during which nests with eggs are likely to be found. Figures in bold type refer to Plate numbers; the last figure refers to the appropriate page in the Species List.

Habitat and Site	Species (page no.)	Remarks	Nesting months
COASTAL HABITATS **Sandy shores** On the ground			
*Arctic Tern **9, 10**	(134)	Scrape with varying amount material (in colonies)	5 6 7
*Avocet **36**	(128)	Scrape often bare (small colonies)	4 5 6
*Black-headed Gull **2**	(131)	Bits of plant material (in colonies)	4 5 6 7
*Common Gull **5**	(131)	Some nests substantial (in colonies)	4 5 6 7
*Common Tern **8**	(133)	Scrape with varying amount material (in colonies)	5 6 7
*Eider **21**	(104)	Often in exposed site	4 5 6 7
*Herring Gull **4**	(131)	Some nests substantial (in colonies)	4 5 6 7
*Kentish Plover **33**	(122)	Shallow scrape	5 6
*Lesser Black-backed Gull **3**	(132)	Nests usually substantial (in colonies)	5 6 7
*Little Tern **11**	(134)	Scrape occasionally decorated	5 6 7
*Oystercatcher **37**	(120)	Scrape often decorated	4 5 6 7
*Red-breasted Merganser **245**	(105)	Nest hidden in cover	5 6 7
*Ringed Plover **31**	(121)	Scrape in the open	4 5 6 7
*Roseate Tern —	(134)	Scrape with varying amount material (in colonies)	6 7
*Sandwich Tern **12**	(133)	Scrape with varying amount material (in colonies)	5 6 7

Habitat and Site	Species (page no.)	Remarks	Nesting months
Shingle Shores On the ground			
*Common Gull **5**	(131)	Some nests substantial (in colonies)	4 5 6 7
*Eider **21**	(104)	Often in exposed site	4 5 6 7
*Great Black-backed Gull **6**	(132)	Nests often substantial (in colonies)	4 5 6
*Herring Gull **4**	(131)	Some nests substantial (in colonies)	4 5 6 7
*Temminck's Stint —	(125)	Usually northern tundra	6 7
Turnstone **222**	(127)	Northern breeding range	5 6
Steep and rocky coasts On the ground			
*Black Guillemot **236**	(136)	Under boulders (isolated pairs or small colonies)	5 6 7
*Black-headed Gull **2**	(131)	Bits of plant material (in colonies)	4 5 6 7
*Common Gull **5**	(131)	Some nests substantial (in colonies)	4 5 6 7
*Eider **21**	(104)	Often in exposed site	4 5 6 7
*Great Black-backed Gull **6**	(132)	Nests often substantial (in colonies)	4 5 6
*Leach's Petrel —	(93)	Remote islands, rock and turf (in colonies)	5 6 7 8
*Lesser Black-backed Gull **3**	(132)	Nests usually substantial (in colonies)	5 6 7
*Puffin **247**	(135)	Burrow excavated (in colonies)	4 5 6 7
*Rock Pipit **176**	(175)	May be at foot of cliff or on top	4 5 6 7
*Snow Bunting **168**	(186)	Northern mountains among scree and boulders	5 6 7
*Storm Petrel —	(92)	Remote parts of Atlantic and Mediterranean coasts (colonies)	5 6 7 8
On rock-faces			
*Chough **216**	(152)	Brittany, Spain, Alps, Wales, S.W. Scotland (in colonies)	4 5 6
*Cormorant **237**	(94)	Ledges and crevices (in colonies)	3 4 5 6 7 8
*Fulmar —	(92)	Precipitous ledges (in colonies)	5 6 7
*Gannet **249**	(93)	Colonies mostly on remote islands	4 5 6 7
*Golden Eagle —	(107)	Scotland, northern Scandinavia, Alps, S. Europe	3 4 5 6
*Guillemot **13, 248**	(135)	Colonies on open ledges	4 5 6 7
*Kittiwake —	(130)	Colonies often large	5 6 7
*Manx Shearwater —	(92)	Colonies on Atlantic and Mediterranean coasts	5 6 7

Habitat and Site	Species (page no.)	Remarks	Nesting Months
*Osprey **244**	(107)	Main breeding distribution East of Baltic Sea	4 5 6
*Peregrine **231**	(112)	Usually in recess towards top of cliff	4 5 6
*Raven **63**	(150)	Ledge or crevice	2 3 4
*Razorbill —	(135)	Colonies usually in sheltered crevices	4 5 6 7
*Rock Dove —	(137)	Several pairs usually in same vicinity	4 5 6 7
*Shag **238**	(94)	May be inside sea-cave (in colonies)	3 4 5 6 7 8
White-tailed Eagle —	(110)	Mainly in far north and E. Europe	3 4

Coastal woodlands
In trees

*Cormorant **237**	(94)	In colonies	3 4 5 6 7 8
*Osprey **244**	(107)	Usually in pine or spruce in Scotland	4 5 6
*Raven **63**	(150)	—	2 3 4
White-tailed Eagle —	(110)	Mainly in far north and E. Europe	3 4

Holes in trees

*Goldeneye —	(107)		4 5

Dunes
On the ground

*Arctic Tern **9, 10**	(134)	Scrape with varying amount material (in colonies)	5 6 7
*Common Gull **5**	(131)	Some nests substantial (in colonies)	4 5 6 7
*Common Tern **8**	(133)	Scrape with varying amount material (in colonies)	5 6 7
*Curlew **41**	(124)	Occasionally on dunes	4 5 6 7
*Eider **21**	(104)	Often in exposed site	4 5 6 7
*Kentish Plover **33**	(122)	Shallow scrape	5 6
*Little Ringed Plover **32, 211**	(121)	Scantily lined scrape	4 5 6 7
*Meadow Pipit **136, 177, 178**	(175)	Nest hidden in cover	4 5 6 7
*Montagu's Harrier **60**	(111)	—	5 6 7
*Oystercatcher **37**	(120)	Scrape often decorated	4 5 6 7
*Pintail **19**	(101)	—	4 5 6 7
*Ringed Plover **31**	(121)	Scrape in the open	4 5 6 7
*Sandwich Tern **12**	(133)	Scrape with varying amount material (in colonies)	5 6 7
*Short-eared Owl **54**	(139)	Builds own nest	3 4 5 6 7
*Stone Curlew —	(129)	—	4 5 6 7 8
Tawny Pipit **173, 174**	(175)	Nest hidden in cover	6

In burrows

*Shelduck **22**	(100)	Often in rabbit burrow	4 5 6 7

Habitat and Site	Species (page no.)	Remarks	Nesting Months
In low thicket			
Scarlet Grosbeak **194**	(183)	Main breeding areas E. Europe	6 7
Greensward			
On the ground			
*Blue-headed Wagtail **137**	(176)	Nest hidden in cover	4 5 6 7
*Common Tern **8**	(133)	Scrape with varying amount material (in colonies)	5 6 7
*Dunlin **44**	(125)	Scrape in vegetation	5 6 7
*Lapwing **38**	(122)	—	3 4 5 6
*Red-breasted Merganser **245**	(105)	Nest hidden in cover	5 6 7
*Redshank **43**	(127)	Nest hidden in cover	4 5 6
*Temminck's Stint —	(125)	Chiefly northern tundra	6 7
Mudflats, shallows and brackish marshes			
On the ground			
*Arctic Skua **250**	(130)	Northern breeding range	5 6 7
*Avocet **36**	(128)	Scrape often bare	4 5 6
*Blue-headed Wagtail **137**	(176)	Nest hidden in cover	4 5 6 7
*Common Scoter —	(104)	Northern breeding range	5 6 7
*Great Skua —	(130)	Northern breeding range	5 6 7
In reedbeds			
*Bearded Reedling **153**	(158)	Nest low above water	4 5 6 7
Estuaries			
On the ground			
*Avocet **36**	(128)	Scrape often bare	4 5 6
*Black-headed Gull **2**	(131)	In colonies	4 5 6 7
*Common Tern **8**	(133)	Scrape with varying amount material (in colonies)	
*Lapwing **38**	(122)		3 4 5 6
*Little Tern **11**	(134)	Scrape usually bare	5 6 7
*Oystercatcher **37**	(120)	Scrape often decorated	4 5 6 7
*Pochard —	(102)	Nest hidden near water	4 5 6 7
*Redshank **43**	(127)	Nest hidden	4 5 6
*Ringed Plover **31**	(121)	Open scrape	4 5 6 7
In burrows			
*Goldeneye —	(104)	Sometimes in rabbit burrow	4 5
*Shelduck **22**	(100)	Often in rabbit burrow	4 5 6 7
In reedbeds			
*Bearded Reedling **153**	(158)	Nest low above water	4 5 6 7
*Grey Lag Goose —	(99)	Nest in old reeds	4 5 6
Squacco Heron **227**	(96)	Southern breeding range	5 6
In trees			
*Goldeneye —	(104)	Nest often some distance from water	4 5
Squacco Heron **227**	(96)	Southern breeding range	5 6

INLAND HABITATS
Reedswamps and freshwater lakes
'Floating' or at ground level

Habitat and Site	Species (page no.)	Remarks	Nesting Months
*Coot **30**	(118)	Nest in scanty cover of reeds	4 5 6 7
*Great Crested Grebe **23**	(90)	—	3 4 5 6 7 8
*Little Grebe —	(91)	—	3 4 5 6 7 8
Red-necked Grebe **233**	(90)	—	5 6
*Slavonian Grebe —	(90)	Northern breeding range	5 6 7

In reeds above water

Aquatic Warbler **157**	(169)	Nest hidden in cover	5 6
*Bearded Reedling **153**	(158)	—	4 5 6 7
*Bittern **240**	(96)	Flat nest	4 5 6
Great Reed Warbler **83**	(168)	Nest suspended in reeds	5 6 7
Little Bittern **26**	(96)	—	5 6 7
*Marsh Harrier **59**	(110)	—	4 5 6 7
*Moorhen **29**	(118)	Nest in dense vegetation	3 4 5 6 7 8
*Reed Warbler **84**	(168)	Nest suspended in reeds	5 6 7 8
*Savi's Warbler **189**	(169)	Nest in dense vegetation	5 6 7
*Sedge Warbler **86**	(169)	Nest in dense vegetation	5 6 7 8
Spoonbill —	(98)	Extensive reedbeds	4 5 6

On the ground

Ferruginous Duck **16, 239**	(103)	Nest hidden close to water	5 6
*Gadwall —	(100)	Nest hidden in cover	5 6
*Grey Lag Goose —	(99)	Nest in old reeds	4 5 6
*Pheasant **49**	(116)	—	4 5 6
Purple Heron **24**	(95)	Southern breeding range (in colonies)	4 5
*Spotted Crake **213**	(119)	Nest in dense vegetation	5 6 7
*Teal —	(101)	Nest hidden in cover	4 5 6

In bushes or trees

*Night Heron —	(95)	Main breeding areas S. and S.E. Europe	5 6

Land vegetation zone near freshwater
On the ground

Baillon's Crake **210**	(120)	Nest hidden in cover	5 6 7
*Black-headed Gull **2**	(131)	In colonies	4 5 6 7
*Black-necked Grebe **234**	(91)	May also be 'floating' (in colonies or singly)	5 6 / 5 6
*Black Tern **7**	(133)	May also be 'floating' (in colonies or singly)	5 6
*Blue-headed Wagtail **137**	(176)	Nest hidden in cover	4 5 6 7
*Common Gull **5**	(131)	Some nests substantial (in colonies)	4 5 6 7

Habitat and Site	Species (page no.)	Remarks	Nesting Months
*Common Tern **8**	(133)	Scrape with varying amount material (in colonies)	5 6 7
Crane —	(116)	—	3 4 5
Ferruginous Duck **16, 239**	(103)	Nest hidden in cover	5 6
*Garganey **18**	(101)	Nest often some distance from water	5 6 7
*Grey Lag Goose —	(99)	Nest in old reeds	4 5 6
*Mute Swan **15**	(99)	Nest often at edge of reedbed	3 4 5 6
*Nightingale **76**	(160)	Nest may be hidden in cover	5 6
*Pintail **19**	(101)	Nest often some distance from water	4 5 6 7
*Pochard —	(102)	Nest hidden in cover	4 5 6 7
*Red-crested Pochard —	(102)	In dense cover	5 6
*Red-spotted Bluethroat —	(161)	—	6 7
*Reed Bunting **144**	(180)	—	4 5 6 7
*Short-eared Owl **54**	(139)	—	3 4 5 6 7
*Shoveler **20**	(102)	Nest hidden in cover	4 5 6
*Snipe **39**	(123)	Nest hidden in cover	4 5 6 7
*Teal —	(101)	Nest often some distance from water	4 5 6
*Tufted Duck —	(103)	Nest hidden in cover (often social)	5 6 7 8
*Water Rail **27, 221**	(119)	Nest often in sedges	4 5 6 7
White-spotted Bluethroat **78, 187**	(160)	Nest hidden in cover	4 5 6
*Wigeon —	(101)	Nest often some distance from water	4 5 6
*Yellow Wagtail **138**	(176)	—	4 5 6 7

Holes or nestboxes in trees

*Goldeneye —	(104)	In old trees	4 5

Shores of freshwater
On the ground

*Common Gull **5**	(131)	In colonies	4 5 6 7
*Common Sandpiper **230**	(125)	Nest may be shingle or vegetation	5 6 5 6
*Dunlin **44**	(125)	—	5 6 7
*Little Ringed Plover **32, 211**	(121)	Nest in shingle or scanty vegetation	4 5 6 7
*Mallard **17**	(100)	—	3 4 5 6 7
*Montagu's Harrier **60, 232**	(111)	Often in rush or sedge	5 6 7
*Red-spotted Bluethroat —	(161)	—	6 7
*Ruff **45**	(124)	Favours marshy ground	5 6
*Scaup —	(103)	Northern breeding range	5 6
White-spotted Bluethroat **78, 187**	(160)	Nest hidden in cover	4 5 6

Habitat and Site	Species (page no.)	Remarks	Nesting Months
*Willow Warbler **95, 253**	(166)	—	
*Wood Sandpiper **218**	(126)	—	5 6
In burrows			
*Bee-eater —	(143)	In low bank or flat ground	5 6
*Kingfisher **130**	(142)	Usually in steep bank	4 5 6 7
Roller —	(143)	Trees in the vicinity	5 6
*Sand Martin **129**	(149)	In colonies	5 6 7
Crevices and niches			
*Dipper —	(158)	Domed nest of moss	3 4 5 6
*Grey Wagtail **139**	(177)	—	4 5 6 7
*Pied Wagtail **192**	(177)	—	4 5 6 7
*White Wagtail **140**	(177)	Often under a bridge	4 5 6 7
In low cover			
Barred Warbler **88**	(171)	—	5 6 7
*Garden Warbler **89, 184**	(171)	—	5 6 7
*Marsh Warbler **85**	(168)	Often in nettles	5 6 7
Scarlet Grosbeak **194**	(183)	Northern and eastern breeding range	6 7
*Sedge Warbler **86**	(169)	In dense cover	5 6 7
In bushes or trees			
*Fieldfare **73**	(164)	In small colonies on Continent	4 5 6
Penduline Tit —	(155)	Often overhanging water	5 6
*Turtle Dove —	(137)	—	5 6 7

Wooded margins of freshwater
On the ground

Habitat and Site	Species	Remarks	Nesting Months
*Black-throated Diver —	(89)	Northern breeding range	5 6 7
*Red-breasted Merganser **245**	(105)	Nest hidden in cover	5 6 7
*Red-throated Diver **14**	(89)	Northern breeding range	5 6 7
*Temminck's Stint —	(125)	Usually northern tundra	6 7
Holes in trees			
*Goosander **246**	(105)	—	4 5 6
In trees			
*Cormorant **237**	(94)	In colonies	3 4 5 6 7 8
*Goldeneye —	(104)	Not always in hole	4 5
*Grey Heron **25**	(94)	In colonies (occasionally single nest)	3 4 5 6 7 8
*Osprey **244**	(107)	Usually in spruce or pine in Scotland	4 5 6
White-tailed Eagle —	(110)	Mainly in far north and E. Europe	3 4

Marshy ground with rank vegetation
On the ground

Habitat and Site	Species	Remarks	Nesting Months
*Canada Goose —	(99)	Often on islet or close to water	3 4 5

Habitat and Site	Species (page no.)	Remarks	Nesting Months
Crane —	(116)	—	3 4 5
*Garganey **18**	(101)	—	5 6 7
*Grasshopper Warbler **82, 190, 252**	(170)	Nest hidden in cover	5 6 7
*Pheasant **49**	(116)	—	4 5 6
*Reed Bunting **144**	(186)	—	4 5 6 7
*Snipe **39**	(123)	Nest hidden in cover	4 5 6 7
*Wigeon —	(101)	Nest often some distance from water	5 6
*Wood Sandpiper **218**	(126)	—	5 6
In bushes or trees			
*Green Sandpiper **219**	(126)	Uses old nests of other species	4 5 6
*Night Heron —	(95)	Main breeding areas S. and S.E. Europe	5 6
*Redwing **206**	(164)	Northern breeding range	5 6 7
Squacco Heron **227**	(96)	Southern breeding range	5 6

Marshy ground and boggy moorland
'Floating' or at ground level

*Slavonian Grebe —	(90)	Northern breeding range	5 6 7
*Water Rail **27, 221**	(119)	Nest hidden in cover	4 5 6 7
On the ground			
*Arctic Skua **250**	(130)	—	5 6 7
Baillon's Crake **210**	(120)	Nest hidden in cover	4 5 6 7
*Black-headed Gull **2**	(131)	—	5 6 7
*Black-tailed Godwit **42**	(124)	Nest hidden in cover	4 5 6
*Black Tern **7**	(133)	Nest surrounded by water	5 6
*Common Gull **5**	(131)	Some nests substantial	4 5 6 7
*Curlew **41**	(124)	—	4 5 6 7
*Dunlin **44**	(125)	—	5 6 7
*Golden Plover **34**	(122)	Often in hummocky terrain	4 5 6 7
*Great Skua —	(130)	Orkney, Shetland, St Kilda	5 6 7
*Greenshank **235**	(126)	Northern breeding range	5 6
*Hen Harrier —	(110)	Nest in open site	4 5 6
Little Crake **28, 212**	(119)	Nest hidden in cover	5 6 7
*Merlin **229**	(112)	—	5 6
*Pintail **19**	(101)	—	4 5 6
*Pochard —	(102)	—	4 5 6 7
*Red Grouse **226**	(114)	—	3 4 5 6
*Red-necked Phalarope **209**	(128)	Northern breeding range	5 6 7
*Red-spotted Bluethroat —	(161)	Sometimes in birch and willow scrub	6 7
*Short-eared Owl **54**	(139)	Favours open site	3 4 5 6 7
*Shoveler **20**	(102)	Nest may be some distance from water	4 5 6
*Spotted Crake **213**	(119)	Nest hidden in cover	5 6 7
*Whimbrel —	(124)	Northern breeding range	5 6
*Whinchat **80**	(162)	Nest at foot of bushy growth	5 6 7

Habitat and Site	Species (page no.)	Remarks	Nesting Months
Willow Grouse **224**	(114)	Northern breeding range	5 6
*Wood Sandpiper **218**	(126)	—	5 6

Damp meadows and fields
On the ground

*Black Grouse **50**	(113)	—	4 5 6 7
*Black-tailed Godwit **42**	(124)	—	4 5 6
*Blue-headed Wagtail **137**	(176)	Nest hidden in cover	4 5 6 7
*Curlew **41**	(124)	—	4 5 6 7
*Grasshopper Warbler **82, 190, 252**	(170)	Nest hidden in cover	5 6 7
*Lapwing **38**	(122)	Favours cultivated ground	3 4 5 6
*Meadow Pipit **136, 177, 178**	(175)	Nest hidden in cover	4 5 6 7
*Ruff **45**	(124)	Favours wet ground	5 6
*Short-eared Owl **54**	(139)	—	3 4 5 6 7
*Snipe **39**	(123)	Nest hidden in cover	4 5 6 7
*Water Rail **27, 221**	(119)	Nest hidden in cover	4 5 6 7
*Whinchat **80**	(162)	—	5 6 7
*Wood Sandpiper **218**	(126)	—	5 6

Small woods by running water
On the ground

Crane —	(116)	—	3 4 5
*Pheasant **49**	(116)	—	4 5 6
River Warbler **81, 191**	(170)	Nest hidden in cover	5 6 7
Thrush Nightingale **186**	(160)	—	5 6

In low undergrowth

Barred Warbler **88**	(171)	At edge of wood	5 6
Scarlet Grosbeak **194**	(183)	Northern and eastern breeding range	6 7

In bushes or trees

*Greenfinch **104**	(180)	At edge of wood	4 5 6 7
*Night Heron —	(95)	In colonies	5 6
*Turtle Dove —	(137)	Comparatively flimsy nest	5 6 7

In trees

*Carrion Crow **64**	(150)	—	3 4 5
*Golden Oriole **110**	(149)	Suspended in fork of branches	5 6
*Goldfinch **101, 160**	(182)	—	5 6 7
*Hooded Crow —	(151)	—	4 5
Lesser Spotted Eagle —	(108)	Secluded forests	5

Holes in trees

Middle Spotted Woodpecker —	(145)	Avoids conifers	4 5 6

Habitat and Site	Species (page no.)	Remarks	Nesting Months
Deciduous woodland			
On the ground			
*Capercaillie **51**	(113)	—	4 5 6
Eagle Owl —	(138)	Nest hidden in cover	4
*Pheasant **49**	(116)	—	4 5 6
*Tree Pipit **135, 179, 180, 255**	(176)	Nest hidden in cover	5 6
*Willow Warbler **95, 253**	(166)	—	5 6
*Wood Warbler **96**	(167)	Nest hidden in cover	5 6
*Woodcock **40**	(123)	—	3 4 5 6 7
Close to the ground			
*Robin **77**	(161)	Nest in hollow or niche	3 4 5 6 7
*Wren **154**	(159)	Nest looks like ball of moss	4 5 6 7
On the ground or in low undergrowth			
*Chiffchaff **94**	(166)	—	4 5 6 7
*Nightingale **76**	(160)	Nest hidden in cover	5 6
*Ring Ouzel **208**	(163)	—	4 5 6 7
In low undergrowth			
*Blackcap **91, 92**	(172)	—	5 6 7
*Dunnock **112**	(174)	Nest includes lots of moss	3 4 5 6 7 8
*Garden Warbler **89, 184**	(171)	—	5 6 7
In bushy cover			
*Long-tailed Tit **147**	(155)	Oval nest decorated with lichen	3 4 5 6
In bushes and trees			
*Blackbird **74**	(163)	—	3 4 5 6 7
*Firecrest **145**	(166)	In branches of conifer	5 6 7
*Greenfinch **104**	(180)	At edge of wood	4 5 6 7
Icterine Warbler **87**	(167)	Usually in fork of branch	5 6
*Jay **68, 256**	(152)	Nest close to tree-trunk	4 5 6
*Song Thrush **75**	(164)	Hard lining to nest, usually light coloured	3 4 5 6 7
In trees			
Black Kite **242**	(109)	—	4 5
Black Stork —	(97)	In old trees	5
*Brambling **102, 167**	(184)	Northern breeding range	5 6
*Buzzard **55**	(108)	Favours edge of wood	4 5 6
*Chaffinch **103, 165, 166**	(184)	Nest thick-walled and felted	4 5 6
*Fieldfare **73**	(164)	At edge of wood	4 5 6
*Golden Oriole **110**	(149)	Suspended in fork of branches	5 6
*Goshawk **56**	(106)	Secluded site	4 5 6
*Hawfinch **97, 98**	(180)	Foundation of dry twigs, not felted	4 5 6 7
*Honey Buzzard **243**	(108)	—	5 6 7
*Long-tailed Tit **147**	(155)	Oval nest decorated with lichen	3 4 5 6

Habitat and Site	Species (page no.)	Remarks	Nesting Months
*Red Kite **241**	(109)	Scattered trees or edge of wood	4 5
Redpoll (Mealy) **99**	(181)	Often in small colonies	5 6 7
*Wood Pigeon **61**	(136)	—	3 4 5 6 7

Crevices and niches in trees

Red-breasted Flycatcher **158**	(173)	Favours beech trees	6
*Redstart **71**	(161)	—	5 6 7
*Short-toed Treecreeper **120**	(156)	—	4 5 6 7
*Spotted Flycatcher **115**	(172)	—	5 6 7
*Treecreeper **152**	(156)	—	4 5 6 7

Holes in trees

*Blue Tit **122, 148**	(153)	—	4 5 6 7
Collared Flycatcher **117**	(173)	—	5 6
*Great Spotted Woodpecker —	(144)	Excavates hole	4 5 6
*Great Tit **121**	(153)	—	4 5 6 7
Grey-headed Woodpecker —	(146)	Avoids conifers	5 6
*Lesser Spotted Woodpecker —	(145)	Excavates hole	4 5 6
*Marsh Tit **124**	(154)	—	4 5 6
Middle Spotted Woodpecker —	(145)	Avoids conifers	4 5 6
*Nuthatch **118**	(157)	Plastered entrance-hole	4 5
*Pied Flycatcher **116**	(173)	—	5 6
Scops Owl —	(139)	—	5 6
*Starling **69**	(179)	—	4 5 6
*Stock Dove —	(136)	—	3 4 5 6 7 8
*Tawny Owl —	(140)	Also in old nests of Birds of Prey	3 4 5
Ural Owl —	(140)	In old trees	3 4 5
White-backed Woodpecker —	(145)	Old beech trees in highland country	4 5
*Wryneck —	(146)	No nesting material in hole	5 6 7

Woodland of mixed species
On the ground

Bonelli's Warbler **155**	(167)	Nest site on sunny slope	5 6
*Capercaillie **51**	(113)	—	4 5 6
Eagle Owl —	(138)	Nest hidden in cover	4
Hazel Hen **223**	(113)	Nest hidden in cover	4 5
*Nightjar **131**	(141)	No nest built	5 6 7 8
*Pheasant **49**	(116)	—	4 5 6
*Tree Pipit **135, 179, 180, 255**	(176)	Nest hidden in cover	5 6
*Willow Warbler **95, 253**	(166)	Nest hidden in cover	5 6

Habitat and Site	Species (page no.)	Remarks	Nesting Months
*Wood Warbler **96**	(167)	Nest hidden in cover	5 6
*Woodcock **40**	(123)	Nest hidden in cover	3 4 5 6 7
Close to the ground			
*Robin **77**	(161)	Nest in hollow or niche	3 4 5 6 7
*Wren **154**	(159)	Nest looks like ball of moss	4 5 6 7
On the ground or in low undergrowth			
*Chiffchaff **94**	(166)	—	4 5 6 7
In low undergrowth			
*Blackcap **91, 92**	(172)	—	5 6 7
*Dunnock **112**	(174)	Nest includes lots of moss	3 4 5 6 7 8
*Garden Warbler **89, 184**	(171)	—	5 6 7
*Long-tailed Tit **147**	(155)	Oval nest decorated with lichen	3 4 5 6
Scarlet Grosbeak **194**	(183)	Northern and eastern breeding range	6 7
In bushes and trees			
*Blackbird **74**	(163)	—	3 4 5 6 7
*Bullfinch **195**	(183)	Usually 1–2 m from ground	4 5 6 7 8
*Firecrest **145**	(166)	In branches of conifer	5 6 7
*Greenfinch **104**	(180)	At edge of wood	4 5 6 7
*Jay **68, 256**	(152)	Nest close to trunk	4 5 6
*Long-eared Owl **62**	(139)	Uses old nests of other species	3 4 5
*Redwing **206**	(164)	Northern breeding range	5 6 7
*Song Thrush **75**	(164)	Hard lining to nest, usually light coloured	3 4 5 6 7
*Turtle Dove —	(137)	Comparatively flimsy nest	5 6 7
In trees			
Black Kite **242**	(109)	Rags and other rubbish in nest	4 5
Booted Eagle —	(108)	Distribution from plains to sub-alpine regions	5
*Brambling **102, 167**	(184)	Northern breeding range	5 6
*Buzzard **55**	(108)	Favours edge of wood	4 5 6
*Chaffinch **103, 165, 166**	(184)	Nest thick-walled and felted	4 5 6
*Honey Buzzard **243**	(108)	—	5 6 7
*Mistle Thrush **207**	(163)	—	3 4 5 6
*Red Kite **241**	(109)	Rags and other rubbish in nest	4 5
Redpoll (Mealy) **99**	(181)	—	5 6 7
Short-toed Eagle —	(109)	Distribution from plains to sub-alpine regions	5
*Wood Pigeon **61**	(136)	—	3 4 5 6 7
Crevices and niches in trees			
Red-breasted Flycatcher **158**	(173)	Favours beech trees	6
*Redstart **71**	(161)	—	5 6 7

Habitat and Site	Species (page no.)	Remarks	Nesting Months
*Spotted Flycatcher 115	(172)	—	5 6 7
Holes in trees			
Black Woodpecker —	(146)	Excavates hole	4 5
*Blue Tit 122, 148	(153)	—	4 5 6 7
*Great Spotted Woodpecker —	(144)	Excavates hole	4 5 6
*Great Tit 121	(153)	—	4 5 6 7
Grey-headed Woodpecker 126	(146)	Avoids conifers	5 6
*Lesser Spotted Woodpecker —	(145)	Excavates hole	4 5 6
*Marsh Tit 124	(154)	—	4 5 6
*Nuthatch 118	(157)	Plastered entrance-hole	4 5
*Pied Flycatcher 116	(173)	—	5 6
*Redstart 71	(161)	—	5 6 7
*Starling 69	(179)	—	4 5 6
*Stock Dove —	(136)	—	3 4 5 6 7 8
*Tawny Owl —	(140)	Also in old nests of Birds of Prey	3 4 5
Ural Owl —	(140)	In old trees	3 4 5
*Willow Tit 151	(154)	Excavates hole	4 5 6
*Wryneck —	(146)	No nesting material	5 6 7

Coniferous woodland

On the ground

Bonelli's Warbler 155	(167)	Nest site on sunny slope	5 6
*Capercaillie 51	(113)	—	4 5 6
Eagle Owl —	(138)	Nest hidden in cover	4
*Nightjar 131	(141)	No nest built	5 6 7 8
*Pheasant 49	(116)	—	4 5 6
*Tree Pipit 135, 179, 180, 255	(176)	Nest hidden in cover	5 6
*Willow Warbler 95, 253	(166)	Nest hidden in cover	5 6

On the ground or close to it

*Robin 77	(161)	Nest in hollow or niche	3 4 5 6 7
*Wren 154	(159)	Nest looks like ball of moss	4 5 6 7

On the ground or in low undergrowth

*Chiffchaff 94	(166)	—	4 5 6 7
*Ring Ouzel 208	(163)	Highland or hilly country	4 5 6 7

In low undergrowth

*Blackcap 91, 92	(172)	—	5 6 7
*Dunnock 112	(174)	Nest includes lots of moss	3 4 5 6 7 8
*Lesser Whitethroat 93	(170)	—	5 6 7

In bushes or trees

*Blackbird 74	(163)	—	3 4 5 6 7
Eagle Owl —	(138)	Nest hidden in cover	4
*Jay 68, 256	(152)	Nest close to trunk	4 5 6
*Long-eared Owl 62	(139)	Use old nests of other species	3 4 5 6
*Song Thrush 75	(164)	Hard lining to nest	3 4 5 6 7

Habitat and Site	Species (page no.)	Remarks	Nesting Months
In trees			
Black Kite **242**	(109)	Rags and other rubbish in nest	4 5
*Brambling **102, 167**	(184)	Northern breeding range	5 6
*Bullfinch **195**	(183)	Usually 1–2 m from ground	4 5 6 7 8
*Buzzard **55**	(108)	Favours edge of wood	4 5 6
*Chaffinch **103, 165, 166**	(184)	Nest thick-walled and felted	4 5 6
*Crossbill **163**	(183)	Favours open plantations in Br. Is.	3 4 5
Eagle Owl —	(138)	Uses old nests of other species	4
*Fieldfare **73**	(164)	—	4 5 6
*Goldcrest **146**	(165)	Nest suspended from twigs	4 5 6 7
*Goshawk **56**	(106)	Secluded site	4 5 6
*Hobby **228**	(111)	Uses old nests of other species	5 6
*Honey Buzzard **243**	(108)	—	5 6 7
*Lesser Redpoll **193**	(181)	—	4 5 6 7
*Mistle Thrush **207**	(163)	—	3 4 5 6
Parrot Crossbill **164**	(184)	Nest in dense branches of pine	3 4
*Peregrine **231**	(112)	Uses old nests of other species on Continent	4 5 6
*Red Kite **241**	(109)	Rags and other rubbish in nest	4 5
*Siskin **162**	(182)	Nest in dense branches	4 5 6 7
*Sparrowhawk **57**	(107)	In clearings or fairly open site	5 6
Waxwing **203**	(178)	Northern breeding range	6 7
*Wood Pigeon **61**	(136)	—	3 4 5 6 7
Crevices and niches in trees			
*Short-toed Treecreeper **120**	(156)	—	4 5 6 7
*Spotted Flycatcher **115**	(172)	—	5 6 7
*Treecreeper **152**	(156)	—	4 5 6 7
Holes in trees			
Black Woodpecker —	(146)	Excavates holes	4 5
*Blue Tit **122, 148**	(153)	—	4 5 6 7
*Coal Tit **150**	(153)	—	4 5 6
*Crested Tit **123, 149**	(154)	—	4 5 6
*Great Spotted Woodpecker —	(144)	Excavates hole	4 5 6
*Great Tit **121**	(153)	—	4 5 6 7
*Nuthatch **118**	(157)	Plastered entrance-hole	4 5
*Pied Flycatcher **116**	(173)	—	5 6
Pygmy Owl —	(140)	Secluded site	4 5
*Redstart **71**	(161)	—	5 6 7
*Starling **69**	(179)	—	4 5 6
*Stock Dove —	(136)	—	3 4 5 6 7 8

Habitat and Site	Species (page no.)	Remarks	Nesting Months
*Tawny Owl —	(140)	Also in old nests of Birds of Prey	3 4 5
Tengmalm's Owl —	(140)	Often in hole made by Black Woodpecker	4 5
Three-toed Woodpecker —	(145)	Northern breeding range	5 6
Ural Owl —	(140)	In old trees	3 4 5
*Willow Tit 151	(154)	Excavates hole	4 5 6
*Wryneck —	(146)	No nesting material	5 6 7

Clearings and rides in woods
On the ground

*Grasshopper Warbler 82, 190, 252	(170)	Nest hidden in cover	5 6 7
*Greenshank 235	(126)	Northern breeding range	5 6
Lesser Spotted Eagle —	(108)	Secluded site	5
*Nightjar 131	(141)	No nest built	5 6 7 8
River Warbler 81, 191	(170)	—	5 6 7
*Skylark 134, 181, 251	(147)	—	3 4 5 6 7
Tawny Pipit 173, 174	(175)	—	6
*Tree Pipit 135, 179, 180, 255	(176)	Nest hidden in cover	5 6
*Woodlark 133, 182	(147)	—	3 4 5 6 7
*Wood Sandpiper 218	(126)	—	5 6

In low undergrowth

Barred Warbler 88	(171)	—	5 6
*Red-backed Shrike 107, 196, 197	(178)	In thorny thicket	5 6
Scarlet Grosbeak 194	(183)	Northern and eastern breeding range	6 7

In bushes or trees

*Green Sandpiper 219	(126)	Uses old nests of other species	4 5 6

Moors and heaths
On the ground

*Black Grouse 50	(113)	—	4 5 6 7
*Black-tailed Godwit 42	(124)	—	4 5 6
*Curlew 41	(124)	—	4 5 6 7
*Grasshopper Warbler 82, 190, 252	(170)	Nest hidden in cover	5 6 7
*Hen Harrier —	(110)	Nest in open site	4 5 6
*Meadow Pipit 136, 177, 178	(175)	Nest hidden in cover	4 5 6 7
*Nightjar 131	(141)	No nest built	5 6 7 8
*Tree Pipit 135, 179, 180, 255	(176)	Favours conifer heaths on Continent	5 6
*Whimbrel —	(124)	Northern breeding range	5 6
Willow Grouse 224	(114)	Northern breeding range	5 6
*Woodlark 133, 182	(147)	—	3 4 5 6 7

Habitat and Site	Species (page no.)	Remarks	Nesting Months
On the ground or in low undergrowth			
*Ring Ouzel **208**	(163)	Highland or hilly country	4 5 6 7
*Twite **159**	(181)	Northern breeding range	5 6
Scrub woodland			
On the ground			
*Pheasant **49**	(116)	—	4 5 6
*Tree Pipit **135, 179, 180, 255**	(176)	—	5 6
*Yellowhammer **142, 169, 254**	(185)	—	4 5 6 7
In low undergrowth			
*Blackcap **91, 92**	(172)	—	5 6 7
*Chiffchaff **94**	(166)	Also nests on the ground	4 5 6 7
*Lesser Whitethroat **93**	(170)	At edge of wood	5 6 7
*Red-backed Shrike **107, 196, 197**	(178)	At edge of wood	5 6
*Whitethroat **90, 183**	(170)	—	5 6 7
In bushes or trees			
*Blackbird **74**	(163)	—	3 4 5 6 7
Great Grey Shrike **106**	(179)	In thorn bush	4 5
*Greenfinch **104**	(180)	—	4 5 6 7
Icterine Warbler **87**	(167)	Decorated with birch bark	5 6
*Long-eared Owl **62**	(139)	Uses old nests of other species	3 4 5 6
*Song Thrush **75**	(164)	Hard lining to nest, usually light coloured	3 4 5 6 7
*Turtle Dove —	(137)	Comparatively flimsy nest	5 6 7
In trees			
Black Kite **242**	(109)	Rags and other rubbish in nest	4 5
*Buzzard **55**	(108)	Favours edge of wood	4 5 6
*Chaffinch **103, 165, 166**	(184)	Nest thick-walled and felted	4 5 6
*Fieldfare **73**	(164)	In small colonies on Continent	4 5 6
*Golden Oriole **110**	(149)	Suspended in fork of branches	5 6
*Honey Buzzard **243**	(108)	At edge of wood	5 6 7
*Sparrowhawk **57**	(107)	By a clearing or ride	5 6
Holes in trees			
*Great Spotted Woodpecker —	(144)	—	4 5 6
*Green Woodpecker —	(145)	Favours deciduous trees	4 5 6
*Starling **69**	(179)	—	4 5 6
*Tree Sparrow **144, 199**	(187)	—	4 5 6 7

40

Habitat and Site	Species (page no.)	Remarks	Nesting Months

Open country with scattered trees and bushes

On the ground

Habitat and Site	Species (page no.)	Remarks	Nesting Months
*Corn Bunting **141, 170**	(185)	Nest towards edge of verge	5 6 7 8
Ortolan Bunting **143**	(186)	—	5 6
*Stonechat **79**	(162)	Nest often on a slope	4 5 6 7
*Willow Warbler **95, 253**	(166)	Nest hidden in cover	5 6
*Yellowhammer **142, 169, 254**	(185)	—	4 5 6 7

In low undergrowth

Habitat and Site	Species (page no.)	Remarks	Nesting Months
Barred Warbler **88**	(171)	Often found near Red-backed Shrike on Continent	5 6
*Cirl Bunting **171**	(185)	—	4 5 6 7
*Lesser Whitethroat **93**	(170)	—	5 6 7
*Linnet **105**	(181)	Often in gorse or thorny thicket	4 5 6 7 8
*Red-backed Shrike **107, 196, 197**	(178)	In thorny thicket	5 6
*Whitethroat **90, 183**	(170)	—	5 6 7

In bushes or trees

Habitat and Site	Species (page no.)	Remarks	Nesting Months
Great Grey Shrike **106**	(179)	In thorn bush	4 5
*Magpie **66**	(151)	Nest often high in crown	3 4 5 6
*Turtle Dove —	(137)	Comparatively flimsy nest	5 6 7

In trees

Habitat and Site	Species (page no.)	Remarks	Nesting Months
*Carrion Crow **64**	(150)	—	3 4 5
*Goldfinch **101, 160**	(182)	—	5 6 7
*Hobby **228**	(111)	Uses old nests of other species	5 6
*Hooded Crow —	(151)	—	3 4 5
*Kestrel **58**	(111)	Uses old nests of other species	4 5 6
Lesser Grey Shrike **108**	(179)	Nest often high in crown	5 6
*Raven **63**	(150)	—	3 4
*Rook **65, 215**	(151)	Nests in colonies	3 4 5
White Stork —	(97)	Favours plenty of water in vicinity	4 5
Woodchat Shrike **109**	(178)	—	5 6

Holes in trees

Habitat and Site	Species (page no.)	Remarks	Nesting Months
*Hoopoe **125, 205**	(144)	Nests also in niches	5 6 7
*Jackdaw **67**	(151)	Nests in colonies	4 5
Roller —	(143)	—	5 6
*Starling **69**	(179)	—	4 5 6

Cattle-sheds or out-buildings

Habitat and Site	Species (page no.)	Remarks	Nesting Months
*Pied Wagtail **192**	(177)	On ledge or in crevice	4 5 6 7
*White Wagtail **140**	(177)	On ledge or in crevice	4 5 6 7

Habitat and Site	Species (page no.)	Remarks	Nesting Months
Dry waste ground			
On the ground			
Crested Lark **132**	(147)	—	4 5 6
Great Bustard **53**	(117)	Bare scrape or scantily lined	4 5
*Great Skua —	(130)	Northern breeding range, mainly in islands	5 6 7
*Hen Harrier —	(110)	Nests among crops on Continent	5 6
Little Bustard —	(117)	Southern breeding range	5 6
Ortolan Bunting **143**	(186)	—	5 6
*Partridge **46**	(115)	Favours fallow fields	4 5 6 7
Pratincole **1**	(129)	Southern breeding range	5 6
*Quail **47**	(115)	—	5 6 7 8
*Red-legged Partridge **48**	(114)	—	4 5 6 7
*Skylark **134, 181, 251**	(147)	—	3 4 5 6 7
*Stone Curlew —	(129)	Eggs laid in open on bare ground	4 5 6 7
*Stonechat **79**	(162)	Favours coarse grass site	4 5 6 7
Tawny Pipit **173, 174**	(175)	—	6
In holes or crevices			
*Wheatear **70, 188**	(162)	Cavity stuffed with lining material	4 5 6 7
In nettles or corn			
*Marsh Warbler **85**	(168)	—	5 6
*Whitethroat **90, 183**	(171)	—	5 6 7
In low undergrowth			
*Twite **159**	(181)	Northern breeding range	5 6
*Whitethroat **90, 183**	(171)	—	5 6 7
Dry pasture			
On the ground			
*Corn Bunting **141, 170**	(185)	Favours edge of verge	5 6 7 8
*Corncrake **220**	(118)	—	5 6 7
Great Bustard **53**	(117)	Bare scrape or scantily lined	4 5
Ortolan Bunting **143**	(186)	Favours edge of verge	5 6
*Partridge **46**	(115)	Favours fallow fields	4 5 6 7
*Quail **47**	(115)	—	5 6 7 8
*Skylark **134, 181, 251**	(147)	—	3 4 5 6 7
*Stonechat **79**	(162)	Nest often on a slope	4 5 6 7
Tawny Pipit **173, 174**	(175)	—	6
Sand and gravel pits or stone quarries			
On the ground			
*Little Ringed Plover **32, 211**	(121)	Favours surrounds of flooded gravel pit	4 5 6 7

Habitat and Site	Species (page no.)	Remarks	Nesting Months
In holes			
*Little Owl —	(140)	—	4 5 6
Rock Sparrow **198**	(188)	—	5 6 7
In burrows			
*Bee-eater —	(143)	Southern breeding range	5 6
*Sand Martin **129**	(149)	In colonies	5 6 7
In low undergrowth			
*Whitethroat **90, 183**	(171)	In nettles or thorny growth	5 6 7

Sunny slopes and vineyards

On the ground

Bonelli's Warbler **155**	(167)	Favours wooded slopes	5 6
*Red-legged Partridge **48**	(114)	—	4 5 6 7
Rock Bunting **172**	(186)	Nest hidden in cover	5 6
*Woodlark **133, 182**	(147)	—	3 4 5 6 7
In low undergrowth			
Barred Warbler **88**	(171)	—	5 6
*Cirl Bunting **171**	(185)	—	4 5 6 7
In stone crevices			
Rock Thrush **204**	(165)	Southern breeding range	5 6

Roadsides and railway embankments

On the ground

Ortolan Bunting **143**	(186)	—	5 6
*Stonechat **79**	(162)	Nest often on a slope	4 5 6 7
*Wheatear **70, 188**	(162)	Also nests in holes	4 5 6 7
*Whinchat **80**	(162)	—	5 6 7
*Yellowhammer **142, 169, 254**	(185)	Favours edge of verge	4 5 6 7
In low undergrowth			
*Cirl Bunting **171**	(185)	—	4 5 6 7
*Linnet **105**	(181)	Often in gorse or thorny thicket	4 5 6 7 8
In bushes or trees			
Great Grey Shrike **106**	(179)	In thorn bush	4 5
*Greenfinch **104**	(180)	—	4 5 6 7
In trees			
*Chaffinch **103, 165, 166**	(184)	Nest thick-walled and felted	4 5 6
*Goldfinch **101, 160**	(182)	—	5 6 7
Lesser Grey Shrike **108**	(179)	Nest often high in crown	5 6
*Serin **100, 156**	(182)	Nest high in side branches	4 5 6 7
Woodchat Shrike **109**	(178)	—	5 6
Holes in trees			
*Tree Sparrow, **114, 199**	(187)	—	4 5 6 7

Habitat and Site	Species (page no.)	Remarks	Nesting Months
Holes of all kinds			
*Little Owl —	(140)	In built-up areas	4 5 6
*Pied Wagtail **192**	(177)	—	4 5 6 7
*Tawny Owl —	(140)	Avenues of old trees	3 4 5
*White Wagtail **140**	(177)	Usually near water	4 5 6 7
Parks and gardens			
On the ground			
*Willow Warbler **95, 253**	(166)	Nest hidden in cover	5 6
Close to the ground			
*Nightingale **76**	(160)	Nest hidden in cover	5 6
*Robin **77**	(161)	Nest in hollow or niche	3 4 5 6 7
*Wren **154**	(159)	Nest looks like ball of moss	4 5 6 7
On the ground or in low undergrowth			
*Chiffchaff **94**	(166)	—	4 5 6 7
*Nightingale **76**	(160)	Nest hidden in cover	5 6
*Redwing **206**	(164)	Northern breeding range	5 6 7
In low undergrowth			
*Blackcap **91, 92**	(172)	—	5 6 7
*Bullfinch **195**	(183)	—	4 5 6 7 8
*Dunnock **112**	(174)	Nest includes lots of moss	3 4 5 6 7 8
*Lesser Whitethroat **93**	(170)	Often in brambles	5 6 7
*Long-tailed Tit **147**	(155)	Oval nest decorated with lichen	3 4 5 6
*Red-backed Shrike **107, 196, 197**	(178)	—	5 6
In bushes or trees			
*Blackbird **74**	(163)	—	3 4 5 6 7
*Collared Dove —	(137)	Comparatively flimsy nest	3 4 5 6 7
*Firecrest **145**	(166)	In branches of conifer	5 6 7
*Greenfinch **104**	(180)	—	4 5 6 7
Icterine Warbler **87**	(167)	Nest decorated with birch fibres	5 6
*Magpie **66**	(151)	Nest often high in crown	3 4 5 6
*Song Thrush **75**	(164)	Hard lining to nest, usually light coloured	3 4 5 6 7
*Turtle Dove —	(137)	Comparatively flimsy nest	5 6 7
In trees			
*Carrion Crow **64**	(150)	—	3 4 5
*Chaffinch **103, 165, 166**	(184)	Nest thick-walled and felted	4 5 6
*Fieldfare **73**	(164)	Often in side branch	4 5 6
*Golden Oriole **110**	(149)	Suspended in fork of branches	5 6
*Goldfinch **101, 160**	(182)	—	5 6 7
*Hawfinch **97, 98**	(180)	Often high in tree	4 5 6 7
*Hooded Crow —	(150)		4 5
*Serin **100, 156**	(182)	Nest high in side branches	4 5 6 7

Habitat and Site	Species (page no.)	Remarks	Nesting Months
*Sparrowhawk **57**	(107)	Favours conifers	5 6
*Wood Pigeon **61**	(136)	—	3 4 5 6 7

Crevices and niches in trees

*Pied Wagtail **192**	(177)	—	4 5 6 7
*Short-toed Tree-creeper **120**	(156)	—	4 5 6 7
*Spotted Flycatcher **115**	(172)	—	5 6 7
*White Wagtail **140**	(177)	Usually near water	4 5 6 7

Niches or holes

*Hoopoe **125, 205**	(144)	Also in heaps of stones	5 6 7
*Redstart **71**	(161)	—	5 6 7

Holes or nestboxes in trees

*Blue Tit **122, 148**	(153)	—	4 5 6 7
*Black Redstart **72**	(161)	—	4 5 6 7
Collared Flycatcher **117**	(173)	—	5 6
*Great Spotted Wood-pecker —	(144)	Excavates hole	4 5 6
*Great Tit **121**	(153)	—	4 5 6 7
*Green Woodpecker —	(145)	Favours deciduous trees	4 5 6
Grey-headed Wood-pecker **126**	(146)	Excavates hole	5 6
*House Sparrow **113, 200**	(187)	—	3 4 5 6 7 8
*Lesser Spotted Woodpecker —	(145)	Excavates hole	4 5 6
*Marsh Tit **124**	(154)	—	4 5 6
Middle Spotted Woodpecker —	(145)	Excavates hole	4 5 6
*Nuthatch **118**	(157)	Plastered entrance-hole	4 5
*Pied Flycatcher **116**	(173)	—	5 6
*Redstart **71**	(161)	—	5 6 7
Scops Owl —	(139)	—	5 6
*Short-toed Treecreeper **120**	(156)	—	4 5 6 7
*Starling **69**	(179)	—	4 5 6
*Stock Dove —	(136)	—	3 4 5 6 7 8
*Tawny Owl —	(140)	Avenues of old trees	3 4 5
*Tree Sparrow **114, 199**	(188)	—	4 5 6 7
*Wryneck —	(146)	No nesting material in hole	5 6 7

Built-up areas
Ledges or crevices on buildings or trees

*Black Redstart **72**	(161)	—	4 5 6 7
*Hoopoe **125, 205**	(144)	—	5 6 7
*House Martin **128**	(148)	Mud nests (in colonies)	5 6 7 8
*House Sparrow **113, 200**	(187)	—	3 4 5 6 7 8
*Jackdaw **67**	(151)	Nests in colonies	4 5
*Pied Wagtail **192**	(177)	—	4 5 6 7

Habitat and Site	Species (page no.)	Remarks	Nesting Months
*Rock Dove —	(137)	Feral stock	3 4 5 6 7
*Starling **69**	(179)	—	4 5 6
*Swift —	(141)	—	5 6 7
*White Wagtail **140**	(177)	—	4 5 6 7
On buildings or trees			
*Kestrel **58**	(111)	Nest may be inside church tower	4 5 6
White Stork —	(97)	On roofs or chimneys	4 5
Inside buildings			
Alpine Swift —	(142)	Tall buildings	5 6
*Barn Owl —	(140)	Often in towers or lofts	3 4 5 6 7 8
*Swallow **127**	(148)	Cattle-sheds (social, not in large colonies)	5 6 7 8
In trees			
*Magpie **66**	(151)	Nest often high in crown	3 4 5 6
*Rook **65, 215**	(151)	In colonies	3 4 5

HIGH MOUNTAINS
Alpine meadows
On the ground

*Black Grouse **50**	(113)	Marshy meadows	5
*Dotterel **35**	(122)	Dry stony ground in alpine zone	5 6 7
*Meadow Pipit **136, 177, 178**	(175)	Nest hidden in cover	5 6 7
*Ptarmigan **52**	(113)	—	5 6 7
Water Pipit **175**	(175)	Meadows with streams	5 6 7

On the ground or in low undergrowth

*Twite **159**	(181)	Northern breeding range	5 6

In conifer trees

Citril Finch —	(183)		4 5

Conifer forests
On the ground or low in trees

Bonelli's Warbler **155**	(167)	Nest site on sunny slope	5 6
Citril Finch —	(183)	—	4 5
*Ring Ouzel **208**	(163)	Nest by the trunk	5 6

In trees

*Crossbill **163**	(183)	Favours spruce	3 4 5
*Lesser Redpoll **193**	(181)	Nest by the trunk (social)	5 6
Nutcracker **214**	(152)	Nest near the trunk	3 4
*Ring Ouzel **208**	(163)	Nest by the trunk	5 6
*Siskin **162**	(182)	Nest in dense branches	4 5 6

In holes

Black Woodpecker —	(146)	—	4 5
Three-toed Woodpecker —	(145)	Nests in rotting wood	5 6
Tengmalm's Owl —	(140)	Often in hole made by Black Woodpecker	4 5

46

Habitat and Site	Species (page no.)	Remarks	Nesting Months
Scree and scrub zone On the ground			
Rock Bunting **172**	(186)	Nests between boulders	5 6
*Rock Partridge **225**	(115)	—	5 6
Snow Finch —	(188)	Nests under boulders	5 6 7
*Wheatear **70, 188**	(162)	Plenty of lining material	5 6
In crevices			
Alpine Accentor **111**	(174)	Nest well hidden	5 6 7
*Black Redstart **72**	(161)	—	4 5 6
*Grey Wagtail **139**	(177)	Nest near water	4 5 6 7
*Ring Ouzel **208**	(163)	—	5 6
Rock Thrush **204**	(165)	Southern breeding range	5 6
*Twite **159**	(181)	Northern breeding range	5 6
*White Wagtail **140**	(177)	Usually near water	4 5 6 7
Steep Crags On rock faces			
Alpine Swift —	(142)	In colonies	5 6
*Chough **216**	(152)	In colonies	4 5
Crag Martin **161**	(149)	In small colonies	5 6
*Golden Eagle —	(107)	—	3 4
Griffon Vulture —	(106)	Southern breeding range	2 3
*House Martin **128**	(148)	Mud nests (in colonies)	5 6 7
*Peregrine **231**	(112)	—	3
*Raven **63**	(150)	—	3 4
In rock crevices			
Alpine Chough **217**	(152)	In colonies	4 5 6
*Chough **216**	(152)	In colonies	4 5
Rock Sparrow **198**	(188)	Southern breeding range	5 6 7
Wallcreeper **119**	(157)	Favours vicinity of mountain streams	5 6

GUIDE TO EGG IDENTIFICATION
according to shape, size and colour

BL = Blue
bl = bluish
CM = Cream
cm = creamy
OL = Olive
ol = olive
SD = Sand
sd = sandy
YW = Yellow
yw = yellowish

BR = Brown
br = brownish
GN = Green
gn = greenish
PK = Pink
pk =pinkish
v/ = variable

BU = Buff
bu = buff
GY = Grey
gy = greyish
RD = Red
rd = reddish
WH = White
wh = whitish

SHAPE				short elliptical
SIZE length/width mm	COLOUR			
	white		coloured	
	unmarked	marked	unmarked	marked
39/31				Kestrel (yw WH)
40/31				Merlin (yw WH)
55/44	Booted Eagle			
57/43				Goshawk (gn WH)
57/45		Black Kite		
57/45		Red Kite		
62/46		Osprey		
72/56	White-tailed Eagle			
76/60	Short-toed Eagle			
77/60		Golden Eagle		

SHAPE				elliptical
SIZE length/width mm	COLOUR			
	white		coloured	
	unmarked	marked	unmarked	marked
32/23		Nightjar (gy WH)		
38/26	Little Grebe (bl WH)			
43/30	Black-necked Grebe (bl WH)			
45/31	Slavonian Grebe			
51/34	Red-necked Grebe			
55/37	Great Crested Grebe			

SHAPE				long elliptical
SIZE length/width mm	COLOUR			
	white		coloured	
	unmarked	marked	unmarked	marked
25/16	Swift			
31/19	Alpine Swift			
31/23	Turtle Dove			
32/24	Collared Dove			
38/29	Stock Dove			
39/29	Rock Dove			
40/29	Wood Pigeon			

SHAPE				short ovate	
SIZE	COLOUR				
length/ width	white		coloured		
mm	unmarked	marked	unmarked	marked	

length/width mm	white unmarked	white marked	coloured unmarked	coloured marked
23/19	Kingfisher			
26/22	Bee-eater			
29/23	Pygmy Owl			
31/27	Scops Owl			
32/26	Tengmalm's Owl			
34/28	Little Owl			
40/32		Sparrowhawk (bl WH)		
40/32	Short-eared Owl			
41/32	Long-eared Owl			
42/33		Hobby (yw WH)		
44/34				Woodcock (BR)
48/39	Tawny Owl			
49/42	Ural Owl			
51/41		Honey Buzzard (yw WH)		
52/38			Ferruginous Duck (BU)	
53/42		Peregrine (yw WH)		
54/38				Stone Curlew (gy)
56/45		Buzzard		
58/43			Goldeneye (bl GN)	
60/50	Eagle Owl			
63/51		Lesser Spotted Eagle		

SHAPE				ovate	
SIZE	COLOUR				
length/ width	white		coloured		
mm	unmarked	marked	unmarked	marked	

length/width mm	white unmarked	white marked	coloured unmarked	coloured marked
14/10				Firecrest (pk YW)
14/10				Goldcrest (yw)
14/11				Long-tailed Tit (wh)
15/12		Coal Tit		
15/12		Bonelli's Warbler		
15/12				Willow Warbler (yw WH)
15/12		Blue Tit		
16/12		Chiffchaff		
16/12		Willow Tit		
16/12		Treecreeper		
16/12		Crested Tit		
16/12				Serin (bl WH)
16/12		Wren		
16/12		Short-toed Treecreeper		

49

SHAPE				ovate
SIZE	COLOUR			
length/ width mm	white		coloured	
	unmarked	marked	unmarked	marked
16/12		Marsh Tit		
16/12				Lesser Redpoll (BL)
16/12				Siskin (bl WH)
16/13		Wood Warbler		
17/13				Citril Finch (bl WH)
17/13		Lesser White-throat		
17/13				Red-breasted Flycatcher (yw WH)
17/13				Redpoll (Mealy) (BL)
17/13				Goldfinch (bl WH)
17/13				Twite (bl WH)
17/13	Sand Martin			
17/13		Aquatic Warbler		
17/14		Great Tit		
18/13			Pied Flycatcher (BL)	
18/13		Sedge Warbler		
18/13				Linnet (bl WH)
18/13			Collared Fly-catcher (BL)	
18/13	House Martin			
18/14				Whitethroat (v/gn GY)
18/14				Grasshopper Warbler (pk)
18/14		Reed Warbler		
18/14				Spotted Flycatcher (gn)
18/14		Bearded Tit		
19/13				Icterine Warbler (pk)
19/14				Red-spotted Bluethroat (gn BL)
19/14			Redstart (bl GN)	
19/14				Blue-headed Wagtail (yw WH)
19/14	Lesser Spotted Woodpecker			
19/14				Marsh Warbler (bl WH)
19/14				White-spotted Bluethroat (gn GY)
19/14				Stonechat (gn GY)
19/14				Orphean Warbler (gn WH)
19/14				Yellow Wagtail (yw WH)
19/14		Swallow		
19/14		Tree Sparrow		
19/14				Reed Bunting (ol BR)
19/14	Black Redstart			
19/15				Grey Wagtail (yw WH)
19/15				Whinchat (gn BL)
19/15				Chaffinch (v/BL)
19/15		Robin		
20/14				Scarlet Grosbeak (BL)
20/15				Brambling (v/BL)
20/15		Crag Martin		
20/15				Blackcap (v/BR)

SHAPE				ovate
SIZE length/width mm	COLOUR			
	white		coloured	
	unmarked	marked	unmarked	marked
20/15		Savi's Warbler		
20/15				Ortolan Bunting (v/pk GY)
20/15				Meadow Pipit (v/gy WH)
20/15		Nuthatch		
20/15			Dunnock (bl GN)	
20/15		River Warbler		
20/15		Garden Warbler		
20/15				Garden Warbler (v/gn WH)
20/15				Greenfinch (bl WH)
20/15				Bullfinch (BL)
20/15		White Wagtail		
20/15		Pied Wagtail		
20/17				Waxwing (bl GY)
21/14				Barred Warbler (gn WH)
21/15	Wryneck			
21/16				Rock Bunting (v/gy WH)
21/16				Tree Pipit (v/gy WH)
21/16				Cirl Bunting (gn)
21/16			Nightingale (ol BR)	
21/16				Yellowhammer (v/bl WH)
21/16			Wheatear (bl WH)	
21/16		Water Pipit		
21/16				Rock Sparrow (yw)
21/16				Rock Pipit (gy WH)
22/14		Woodlark		
22/16				Thrush Nightingale (bl WH)
22/16		Tawny Pipit		
22/16				Crossbill (gn)
22/16				Great Reed Warbler (bl WH)
22/17				Snow Bunting (yw WH)
23/16		House Sparrow		House Sparrow (v/gy WH)
23/17		Crested Lark		
23/17				Woodchat Shrike (v/gn)
23/17				Red-backed Shrike (v/gn)
23/17				Parrot Crossbill (gn)
23/17			Alpine Accentor (bl GN)	
23/17	Snow Finch			
23/18	Middle Spotted Woodpecker			
24/17		Skylark		Skylark (v/yw)
24/18		Corn Bunting		
25/18				Hawfinch (gy GN)
25/18	Three-toed Woodpecker			
25/18				Lesser Grey Shrike (GN)
25/19	Dipper			
26/19	Great Spotted Woodpecker			
26/19				Redwing (gn)

SHAPE				ovate	
SIZE length/ width mm	**COLOUR**				
	white		coloured		
	unmarked	marked	unmarked	marked	
26/19				Hoopoe (gn GY)	
26/19		Great Grey Shrike			
26/20			Rock Thrush (gn BL)		
27/20				Song Thrush (gn BL)	
28/20	Grey-headed Woodpecker				
28/20	White-backed Woodpecker				
28/21		Storm Petrel			
29/21				Blackbird (gn BL)	
29/21				Fieldfare (gn BL)	
29/21				Baillon's Crake (yw BR)	
30/21			Starling (BL)		
30/22				Ring Ouzel (gn BL)	
31/21				Golden Oriole (pk WH)	
31/22				Little Crake (yw BR)	
31/22				Mistle Thrush (gn BL)	
31/23	Green Wood- pecker				
32/23				Jay (gn GY)	
33/24				Little Tern (sd)	
34/24				Spotted Crake (yw BR)	
34/24				Magpie (v/gn BL)	
34/25				Jackdaw (bl GN)	
34/25				Nutcracker (bl GN)	
35/25				Black Tern (yw BR)	
35/26	Black Woodpecker				
35/27	Little Bittern				
35/28	Roller				
36/26				Water Rail (cm WH)	
37/26		Alpine Chough			
38/29			Squacco Heron (gn BL)		
39/28				Chough (cm WH)	
39/31	Barn Owl				
40/27				Corncrake (yw WH)	
40/29				Arctic Tern (v/bu OL)	
41/28				Rook (bl GN)	
41/30				Common Tern (bu OL)	
42/33	Montagu's Harrier				
43/30				Carrion Crow (gn BL)	
43/31				Moorhen (BU)	
44/30				Hooded Crow (gn BL)	
44/30				Roseate Tern (v/BU)	
45/33			Garganey (cm BU)		
45/36	Hen Harrier				
46/34			Teal (bu GN)		
46/34			Little Egret (gn BL)		
49/35			Night Heron (gn BL)		
49/38	Marsh Harrier				

SHAPE				ovate
SIZE length/ width mm	**COLOUR**			
	white		coloured	
	unmarked	marked	unmarked	marked
50/33				Raven (gn BL)
50/36				Black Grouse (yw)
52/36				Sandwich Tern (v/yw WH)
52/37			Shoveler (gn GY)	
52/37			Pintail (gn YW)	
52/37				Black-headed Gull (v/gn)
52/38			Gadwall (cm BU)	
52/38			Bittern (ol BR)	
52/39				Little Bustard (ol GN)
52/39				Coot (gy BR)
54/38			Wigeon (cm BU)	
55/40			Purple Heron (gn BL)	
55/40				Kittiwake (v/bl GY)
56/40				Oystercatcher (bu GY)
57/40				Arctic Skua (ol BR)
58/40			Mallard (v/gn)	
58/40				Black Guillemot (v/bl GN)
58/42				Capercaillie (yw)
58/42			Red-crested Pochard (yw GY)	
59/42				Common Gull (v/bl GN)
60/41			Tufted Duck (gn GY)	
60/42			Grey Heron (gn BL)	
61/42	Manx Shearwater			
61/42		Puffin		
61/44			Pochard (gn GY)	
63/43			Scaup (gn GY)	
65/49	Black Stork			
66/45			Common Scoter (v/cm BU)	
66/45			Red-breasted Merganser (bu OL)	
66/46			Goosander (cm WH)	
66/48			Shelduck (cm WH)	
67/46				Lesser Black-backed Gull (v/gn GY)
68/46		Spoonbill		
71/49				Herring Gull (v/gy BR)
71/49				Great Skua (gy BR)
71/52	White Stork			
74/51	Fulmar			
77/54				Great Black-backed Gull (v/gy BR)
78/50			Gannet (bl GN)	
78/52			Eider (v/gn GY)	
79/56				Great Bustard (v/gy GN)
85/58			Grey Lag Goose (cm WH)	
86/58			Canada Goose (cm WH)	
92/70	Griffon Vulture			
97/61				Crane (ol GN)
115/74			Mute Swan (gy GN)	

SHAPE			long ovate	
SIZE	COLOUR			
length/ width	white		coloured	
mm	unmarked	marked	unmarked	marked

16/11   Penduline Tit

21/14   Wallcreeper

63/38   Shag (BL)

66/41   Cormorant (BL)

74/46   Red-throated Diver (ol BR)

85/53   Black-throated Diver (ol BR)

SHAPE			short pointed ovate	
SIZE	COLOUR			
length/ width	white		coloured	
mm	unmarked	marked	unmarked	marked

46/36   Pheasant (ol BR)

SHAPE			pointed ovate	
SIZE	COLOUR			
length/ width	white		coloured	
mm	unmarked	marked	unmarked	marked

30/23   Quail (yw WH)

36/27   Partridge (ol BR)

41/29   Hazel Hen (rd YW)

41/30   Red Grouse (yw)

41/30   Ptarmigan (yw)

41/31   Rock Partridge (yw WH)

41/31   Red-legged Partridge (yw BR)

43/31   Willow Grouse (yw)

SHAPE			long pointed ovate	
SIZE	COLOUR			
length/ width	white		coloured	
mm	unmarked	marked	unmarked	marked

41/29   Dotterel (ol BR)

54

SHAPE			short pyriform	
SIZE	COLOUR			
length/ width	white		coloured	
mm	unmarked	marked	unmarked	marked

47/34   Lapwing (ol BR)

SHAPE			pyriform	
SIZE	COLOUR			
length/ width	white		coloured	
mm	unmarked	marked	unmarked	marked

28/20   Temminck's Stint
                                                             (gn GY)
30/21   Red-necked
                                                             Phalarope
                                                             (gn GY)
30/22   Little Ringed
                                                             Plover (BU)
33/24   Kentish Plover
                                                             (BU)
34/25   Dunlin (v/bl GN)
36/26   Ringed Plover (BU)
36/26   Common Sand-
                                                             piper (yw BR)
38/27   Wood Sandpiper
                                                             (gn)
39/28   Green Sandpiper
                                                             (gn)
39/29   Snipe (ol BR)
40/29   Turnstone (gy GN)
44/31   Redshank (BU)
45/31   Ruff (v/ol BR)
51/35   Avocet (BU)
52/36   Golden Plover
                                                             (v/cm BU)
55/38   Black-tailed
                                                             Godwit (ol BR)
58/42   Whimbrel (ol BR)
67/47   Curlew (ol BR)

SHAPE			long pyriform	
SIZE	COLOUR			
length/ width	white		coloured	
mm	unmarked	marked	unmarked	marked

51/35   Greenshank
                                                             (yw BR)
73/47   Razorbill (v/)
82/50   Guillemot (v/)

55

Pratincole

2 Black-headed Gull

Lesser Black-backed Gull

4 Herring Gull

Common Gull

6 Great Black-backed Gull

7 Black Tern

8 Common Tern

9 Arctic Tern

10 Arctic Tern

11 Little Tern

12 Sandwich Tern

13 Guillemot

14 Red-throated Diver

15 Mute Swan

16 Ferruginous Duck

17 Mallard

18 Garganey

19 Pintail

20 Shoveler

21 Eider

22 Shelduck

23 Great Crested Grebe

24 Purple Heron

25 Grey Heron

26 Little Bittern

27 Water Rail

28 Little Crake

29 Moorhen

30 Coot

31 Ringed Plover

32 Little Ringed Plover

33 Kentish Plover

34 Golden Plover

35 Dotterel

36 Avocet

37 Oystercatcher

38 Lapwing

39 Snipe

40 Woodcock

41 Curlew

42 Black-tailed Godwit

43 Redshank

44 Dunlin

45 Ruff

46 Partridge

47 Quail

48 Red-legged Partridge

49 Pheasant

50 Black Grouse

51 Capercaillie

52 Ptarmigan

53 Great Bustard

54 Short-eared Owl

55 Buzzard

56 Goshawk

57 Sparrowhawk

58 Kestrel

59 Marsh Harrier

60 Montagu's Harrier

Wood Pigeon

62 Long-eared Owl

Raven

64 Carrion Crow

Rook

66 Magpie

67 Jackdaw

68 Jay

69 Starling

70 Wheatear

71 Redstart

72 Black Redstart

73 Fieldfare

74 Blackbird

75 Song Thrush

76 Nightingale

77 Robin (with Cuckoo's egg)

78 White-spotted Bluethroat

79 Stonechat

80 Whinchat

81 River Warbler

82 Grasshopper Warbler

83 Great Reed Warbler

84 Reed Warbler

85 Marsh Warbler (+ Cuckoo's egg)

86 Sedge Warbler

87 Icterine Warbler

88 Barred Warbler

89 Garden Warbler

90 Whitethroat

91 Blackcap

92 Blackcap

93 Lesser Whitethroat

94 Chiffchaff

95 Willow Warbler

96 Wood Warbler

97 Hawfinch

98 Hawfinch

99 Redpoll

100 Serin

101 Goldfinch

102 Brambling

103 Chaffinch

104 Greenfinch

105 Linnet

106 Great Grey Shrike

107 Red-backed Shrike

108 Lesser Grey Shrike

109 Woodchat Shrike

110 Golden Oriole

111 Alpine Accentor

112 Dunnock

113 House Sparrow

114 Tree Sparrow

115 Spotted Flycatcher

116 Pied Flycatcher

117 Collared Flycatcher

118 Nuthatch

119 Wallcreeper

120 Short-toed Treecreeper

21 Great Tit

122 Blue Tit

23 Crested Tit

124 Marsh Tit

25 Hoopoe

126 Grey-headed Woodpecker

127 Swallow

128 House Martin

129 Sand Martin

130 Kingfisher

131 Nightjar

132 Crested Lark

133 Woodlark

134 Skylark

135 Tree Pipit

136 Meadow Pipit

137 Blue-headed Wagtail

138 Yellow Wagtail

139 Grey Wagtail

140 White Wagtail

141 Corn Bunting

142 Yellowhammer

143 Ortolan Bunting

144 Reed Bunting

145 Firecrest, 146 Goldcrest, 147 Long-tailed Tit, 148 Blue Tit, 149 Crested Tit, 150 Coal Tit, 151 Willow Tit, 152 Treecreeper, 153 Bearded Tit, 154 Wren, 155 Bonelli's Warbler, 156 Serin, 157 Aquatic Warbler, 158 Red-breasted Flycatcher, 159 Twite, 160 Goldfinch, 161 Crag Martin, 162 Siskin, 163 Crossbill, 164 Parrot Crossbill, 165 and 166 Chaffinch, 167 Brambling, 168 Snow Bunting, 169 Yellowhammer, 170 Corn Bunting, 171 Cirl Bunting, 172 Rock Bunting, 173 and 174 Tawny Pipit, 175 Water Pipit, 176 Rock Pipit, 177 and 178 Meadow Pipit, 179 and 180 Tree Pipit, 181 Skylark, 182 Woodlark, 183 Whitethroat, 184 Garden Warbler, 185 Orphean Warbler, 186 Thrush Nightingale, 187 Bluethroat, 188 Wheatear

189 Savi's Warbler, 190 Grasshopper Warbler, 191 River Warbler, 192 Pied Wagtail, 193 Lesser Redpoll, 194 Scarlet Grosbeak, 195 Bullfinch, 196 and 197 Red-backed Shrike, 198 Rock Sparrow, 199 Tree Sparrow, 200 House Sparrow, 201 Cuckoo (leaf warbler type), 202 Cuckoo (reed warbler type), 203 Waxwing, 204 Rock Thrush, 205 Hoopoe, 206 Redwing, 207 Mistle Thrush, 208 Ring Ouzel, 209 Red-necked Phalarope, 210 Baillon's Crake, 211 Little Ringed Plover, 212 Spotted Crake, 213 Little Crake

214 Nutcracker, 215 Rook, 216 Chough, 217 Alpine Chough, 218 Wood Sandpiper, 219 Green Sandpiper, 220 Corncrake, 221 Water Rail, 222 Turnstone, 223 Hazel Hen, 224 Willow Grouse, 225 Rock Partridge

226 Red Grouse, 227 Squacco Heron, 228 Hobby, 229 Merlin, 230 Common Sandpiper, 231 Peregrine, 232 Montagu's Harrier, 233 Red-necked Grebe, 234 Black-necked Grebe

235 Greenshank, 236 Black Guillemot, 237 Cormorant, 238 Shag, 239 Ferruginous
Duck, 240 Bittern

241 Red Kite, 242 Black Kite, 243 Honey Buzzard, 244 Osprey, 245 Red-breasted
Merganser, 246 Goosander

247 Puffin, 248 Guillemot, 249 Gannet, 250 Arctic Skua

251 Skylark

252 Grasshopper Warbler

253 Willow Warbler

254 Yellowhammer

255 Tree Pipit

256 Jay

SPECIES LIST

DIVERS
Gaviidae

Associated with secluded expanses of water in the north, such as highland lochs and lakes in forests. Nests are along the banks or on grassy islets in the water. There is no formal nest construction. The eggs lie in the centre of a heap of flattened vegetation; varying amounts of local plants and moss are added and sometimes the mound is conspicuous. Ground colour of eggs is olive-brown, marked with typical scattering of dark flecks. One brood per year. Clutch-size usually 2. There are two breeding species in northern Europe; both breed regularly in Br. Is. (Great Northern Diver *Gavia immer* may also breed occasionally in Scotland.)

Black-throated Diver* *Gavia arctica*
(Not illustrated)

Site near large lakes in northern forests or by moorland lochs. Nests are usually along the banks, also on promontories and grassy islets surrounded by deep water.

Nest flattened vegetation provides foundation for a central depression. In shallow water nests tend to be built up with plants and moss into a larger mound.

Eggs 2, long ovate; olive-brown to dark brown with scattered markings of very dark flecks. Size 85·4 × 52·8 mm. Weight 122 g. Incubation 28–30 days. Single brood, May–June/July. Replacement clutch.

Nestlings dense greyish down. Distinguished from next species only by larger size. Leave nest shortly after hatching.

Red-throated Diver* *Gavia stellata*
Pl. **14**

Site similar to previous species but favours smaller lochs in Scottish Highlands, particularly when there are more extensive sheets of water near by.

Nest similar to previous species but heap of vegetation tends to be larger.

Eggs 2, long ovate; olive-brown with scattering of dark flecks. Size 74·0 × 45·8 mm. Weight 80 g. Incubation 26–27 (30?) days. Single brood, late May–June/July.

Nestlings dense greyish down, very similar to previous species except for smaller size. Leave nest shortly after hatching.

Associated with reedbeds or similar vegetation in water where there is little or no current. Nests are made out of aquatic plants plastered with mud, forming a damp mound of decaying vegetation with a shallow depression in the centre. When first laid the eggs are white or bluish-white but they soon become discoloured, looking dirty brown or rust-stained. Some species have only one brood, others have two. Clutch-size normally 4–5. Of the five breeding species, Slavonian Grebe does not breed in central Europe and Red-necked Grebe does not breed in Br. Is.

Great Crested Grebe* *Podiceps cristatus*
Pl. **23**

Site usually in dense cover of reeds and rushes in water but also on reservoirs and pools, including gravelpits, where vegetation is less well-established.

Nest a large pile of rotting vegetation plastered with wet mud, built on foundation of reeds or other stems. About one-third of 'floating' heap projects above the water; the centre is smoothed into a shallow depression for the eggs which are usually covered with nesting material before the nest is left unguarded. Found in colonies in southern Europe. Nest diameter 30–60 cm, height usually 15–25 cm but may be up to 30 cm.

Eggs 2–6; white or bluish-white at first, soon discoloured with dark stains. Size 55·2 × 36·6 mm. Weight approx. 38 g. Incubation 25–28 days. One brood per year on the Continent, April–June, two broods in Br. Is., late February–August. Replacement clutch.

Nestlings short down, black and brown striped appearance with small bare patches of reddish skin near eyes and on head. Frequently nestle among feathers of parents who carry them when swimming or in flight.

Red-necked Grebe *Podiceps griseigena*
Pl. **233**

Site in reedbeds and other dense cover of remote stretches of still water, sometimes in secluded forests but also in more open country.

Nest similar to Great Crested, a 'floating' heap of sodden vegetation smoothed into shallow depression in centre. Diameter about 35 cm.

Eggs 4–5, occasionally 7; white or bluish-white, soon discoloured by dark stains. Size 50·5 × 34·0 mm. Weight 30·5 g. Incubation 22–23 days. Usually one brood per year in May, sometimes two. Replacement clutch.

Nestlings black stripes on head. Leave nest shortly after hatching.

Slavonian Grebe* *Podiceps auritus*
(Not illustrated)

Site favours cover of reeds and sedges in shallow water but also on moorland lochs where there is comparatively little vegetative cover. Breeds in northern Europe, including Scotland.

Nest 'floating' heap of damp, rotting vegetation, smoothed into a shallow depression in the centre. Diameter usually 30–40 cm, height about 5–10 cm.

Eggs 3, more rarely 4–6; white or bluish-white, soon discoloured by dark stains. Size 44·5 × 30·7 mm. Weight 19–25 g. Incubation 22–24 days. Single brood, May–June/July.

Nestlings similar to Black-necked but stripes on head, throat and upperparts are well-defined, more like young Great Crested. Leave nest within hours of hatching and can swim at once.

Black-necked Grebe* *Podiceps nigricollis*
Pl. **234**

Site usually in thick cover of reeds and rushes growing in shallow water. Large colonies are found on the Continent and this species is very sociable during breeding season. Nests are also found in colonies of terns and gulls. (Breeds irregularly in Br. Is.)

Nest 'floating' mound of sodden plants and mud with depression in the centre. Diameter about 25–32 cm.

Eggs 3–4, but sometimes 6; bluish-white but soon discoloured by dark stains. Size 43·1 × 29·7 mm. Weight 21 g. Incubation 20–21 days. Single brood, April/May–June/July. Replacement clutch.

Nestlings short down, black and grey striped appearance, bare patch of red skin on forehead. Carried on backs of parents.

Little Grebe* *Podiceps ruficollis*
(Not illustrated)

Site associated with freshwater (still or slow-flowing) where there is plenty of vegetative cover available. Territory around nest, defended against intruders, extends for 1–3 m but may be as much as 5 m from edge of water.

Nest 'floating' mound of damp and decaying plants, sometimes looking like a mere soup-plate. Diameter about 45 cm, height about 11·5 cm.

Eggs generally 5–6, occasionally 4 or 7; bluish-white but soon become discoloured by dark stains. Size 37·8 × 26·2 mm. Weight 13–14 g. Incubation 20–21 days. Two broods per year, occasionally three, peak season May–July. Replacement clutch.

Nestlings black down with lighter stripes, some white on forehead. Able to swim and dive after a few days, also carried on backs of parents.

PETRELS AND SHEARWATERS *Procellariidae*

Nesting colonies are associated with steep sea-cliffs, usually on inaccessible ledges (Fulmar), and with rocky islands where there are holes under boulders or the earth is suitable for excavating burrows (Manx Shearwater). One whitish egg is laid on bare ground; there is virtually no nesting material. One brood per year. Main breeding colonies are in northern Europe, including Br. Is.

Manx Shearwater* *Puffinus puffinus*
(Not illustrated)

Site rocky turf on cliffs or cliff-tops, usually on comparatively remote islands, where there are natural holes under boulders or the earth is suitable for excavation. Burrows may be excavated by the shearwaters or taken over from rabbits. Some colonies are very large.

Nest a mere scrape at the end of a burrow. Sometimes there are a few bits of grass or bracken in the nesting chamber but there is no sign of any construction.

Egg 1; matt white, becomes stained. Size 60·9 × 41·9 mm. Weight 57 g. Incubation 51–61 days. Single brood, May–July. Replacement clutch.

Nestling fed by parents for 8–9 weeks, then abandoned and after approximately 2 weeks it makes its own way to sea.

Fulmar* *Fulmarus glacialis*
(Not illustrated)

Site nearly always inaccessible niches on cliffs overlooking the sea; occasionally on inland crags, and also recorded on buildings and on flat cliff-tops. Colonies in northern Europe and Br. Is.

Nest egg laid on bare ground in shallow niche; no nesting material but some nests are decorated with small stones.

Egg 1; matt white, becomes dirty. Size 74·0 × 50·6 mm. Weight 98 g. Incubation occasionally 52 days, usually 53–57. Single brood, May–July. No replacement clutch.

Nestling white down on head and on underparts, upperparts grey. Leaves nest after about 46 days.

STORM PETRELS   *Hydrobatidae*

Nesting colonies are nearly all on small rocky islands where there are natural holes and crevices, including stone walls, some holes are excavated by the petrels. There is little or no nesting material. One white egg, marked with brown flecks which tend to be concentrated at one end. One brood per year. Breeding colonies are in northern Europe, including the Br. Is.; Storm Petrel colonies are also found in parts of the Mediterranean.

Storm Petrel* *Hydrobates pelagicus*
(Not illustrated)

Site islands with rocks and turf with many natural holes and crevices, including derelict stone buildings and walls. Some holes are excavated by the petrels.

Nest a mere scrape, often without any material but sometimes a few bits of dry vegetation are found in the nesting chamber.

Egg 1; white with small brownish-red or purple flecks. Size 27·9 × 21·2 mm. Incubation 38–41 days. Single brood, late May–mid-

August. Replacement clutch (?). Nestling silver-grey down. Deserted by parents and makes its own way to sea after 8–9 weeks.

Leach's Petrel* *Oceanodroma leucorrhoa*
(Not illustrated)
Site similar to Storm Petrel. Colonies are mainly on islands off N.W. Scotland, Faroe Isles and Iceland.
Nest similar to Storm Petrel.
Egg similar to Storm Petrel but larger. Size 33 × 24 mm. Incubation 41–42 days. Single brood, late May–mid-August.
Nestling slightly larger than Storm Petrel, otherwise similar. Deserted by parents and makes its own way to sea after 9–10 weeks.

GANNETS   *Sulidae*

Large breeding colonies are on precipitous cliffs and slopes, nearly always on remote islands. The nests are mounds of seaweed with bits of local flotsam added. There is usually a single egg which looks whitish, due to chalky deposit on the blue-green shell. Breeding colonies are in northern Europe, including Br. Is.

Gannet* *Sula bassana*
Pl. **249**

Site niches on precipitous cliffs and lower slopes where the ground is often strewn with boulders. Density of nests may be so great that there is barely room to walk between them.
Nest a mound of rotting seaweed; various bits of flotsam lying around may be added. Diameter about 60–70 cm. Height about 28–32 cm.

Egg 1, ovate; blue-green colour whitened by chalky deposit, but egg soon becomes stained. Size 78·1 × 49·1 mm. Weight 106 g. Incubation 44 days. Single brood, peak season May–June.
Nestling white down, sparse at first, showing bare patches of black skin. Deserted by parents and makes its own way to sea after about 75 days.

CORMORANTS   *Phalacrocoracidae*

Breeding colonies are on rocky ledges and boulder-strewn slopes of sea cliffs, sometimes on sloping slabs of rock in caves overlooking the sea. Shag and Cormorant colonies are usually on lower slopes of cliffs. On the Continent, colonies of Cormorant nests are regularly found in tall trees. In Br. Is. there are a few Cormorant colonies on inland crags near freshwater. Seaweed, sticks and twigs form the foundation of the nest, plants and flotsam are sometimes added. There are usually 3–5 eggs, pale blue ground colour but there is a chalky deposit on the shell. Usually one brood per year. Of the two breeding species, both breed in Br. Is. but the Shag does not breed in central Europe.

Cormorant* *Phalacrocorax carbo*
Pl. **237**

Site sea-cliffs with rock ledges and slabs, and lower slopes strewn with boulders, are typical of nesting colonies in Br. Is. Other sites include tall trees (beech, oak, poplar, willow) and thickets of reeds and sedge. Nests are built only a foot or two apart.

Nest a mound of sticks and seaweed, sometimes various bits of flotsam or debris are incorporated. Material may include grass, straw, rushes and fresh green twigs.

Eggs 3–4, rarely 6, long ovate; pale blue with chalky deposit. Size 65·8 × 40·7 mm. Weight 57 g. Incubation 23–24 days. Usually a single brood, but late nests suggest possibility of second brood, March/April—July/August.

Nestlings naked blackish skin at first, later covered with dark brown down. Able to fly after about 4 weeks.

Shag* *Phalacrocorax aristotelis*
Pl. **238**

Site similar to Cormorant. Cormorants and Shags are usually in separate colonies although the same kind of site (rock ledges and crevices) may be shared. Sometimes the Shag colony is on the lowest part of the cliff, near or inside sea-cave.

Nest similar to Cormorant.

Eggs 2–5, long ovate; pale blue with chalky deposit, similar to Cormorant except for smaller size. Size 62·9 × 38·4 mm. Weight 51 g. Incubation 30–31 days. Single brood usually, but extended season in some areas suggests possibility of second brood, March or earlier–July or August. Replacement clutch.

Nestlings naked at first, followed by light brown down. Able to fly after about 4 weeks.

HERONS AND BITTERNS   *Ardeidae*

Nests are of simple construction, looking like untidily arranged layers of branches, sticks, reeds or similar vegetation. They may be colonial or solitary and at heights varying from ground-level to high up in tall trees. Clutch-size is usually 4–5; the eggs are unmarked, matt greenish-blue (Herons), matt olive-brown (Bittern), dull chalky-white (Little Bittern). There is only one brood per year. Seven species breed in central Europe; Grey Heron and Bittern breed regularly in Britain, Night Heron breeds in Edinburgh Zoo and Little Bittern is suspected sporadic breeder in East Anglia.

Grey Heron* *Ardea cinerea*
Pl. **25**

Site frequently in deciduous woodland (oak, beech, alder), sometimes in conifers (spruce, pine), and less frequently on marshes, in reedbeds or bushes of willow and tamarisk. Heron-

ries in trees are often in the top
canopy (15–24 m); solitary nests
are usually in lower half of
canopy.
Nest untidy arrangement of dead
sticks, twigs or reeds, lined with
finer twigs, grass and other plant
material. Diameter about 80–
120 cm.
Eggs 4–6, though sometimes only
3; matt greenish-blue. Size 59·9
× 42·4 mm. Weight about 60 g.
Incubation 25–26 days, occasionally 28. Single brood usually,
peak season March–May.
Nestlings down grey on upper
parts, whitish on under parts,
crested appearance on crown.
Able to fly after 7–8 weeks.

Purple Heron *Ardea purpurea*
Pl. **24**

Site extensive reedbeds and
marshes or swamps with thickets
of willow. Colonies of nests are
usually in dense reeds, sometimes
in bushes and only occasionally in
trees or dead tree-stumps. Height
above water usually only 1 m.
Nest untidy 'platform' of broken
reeds or stems; diameter about
55–80 cm, height about 30 cm,
depression in the centre about
6–10 cm deep.
Eggs 4–5, occasionally 6; greenish-blue, which is a stronger
colour than previous species.
Size 54·7 × 40·0 mm. Weight
51 g. Incubation 26–30 days.
Single brood late April–June. Replacement clutch.
Nestlings sparser down than previous species. Able to fly after
about 7 weeks.

Little Egret *Egretta garzetta*
(Not illustrated)

Site on dry ground as well as on
marshes, in tall trees (oak, elm,
poplar, pine) and in bushes
(willow, tamarisk). Nesting colonies of Little Egret are found on
their own or among other heron-
ries; also gregarious with other
species, Rooks and Birds of Prey
may have nests in part of the
colony.
Nest untidily arranged twigs or
branches; some 'platforms' look
decidedly flimsy, others are made
of coarser material. Diameter
about 33 cm.
Eggs 3–6; pale greenish-blue.
Size 45·8 × 33·8 mm. Weight
28 g. Incubation 21–22, sometimes 25 days. Single brood, late
April–July. Replacement clutch.
Nestlings white down. Able to fly
after about 30 days.

Night Heron* *Nycticorax nycticorax*
(Not illustrated)

Site many colonies are on swampy
ground in trees or bushes (willow,
alder, oak) at a height of 1–6 m
above the water. This species
favours marshes and swamps,
associating freely during the
breeding season with birds like
Spoonbill as well as with other
Herons. (Free-flying birds have
established a breeding colony in
Edinburgh Zoo.)
Nest made out of dry branches
and twigs (willow, etc.) or reeds
and sedge, lined with finer material (grass, rootlets and leaves).
Eggs sometimes only 3, usually
4–5; greenish-blue. Size 48·7 ×

35·3 mm. Weight 36 g. Incubation 21 days. Single brood, May–June. Replacement clutch. *Nestlings* buff and cream-coloured down, crested appearance on head. Able to fly after 3–4 weeks.

Squacco Heron *Ardeola ralloides*
Pl. **227**

Site many nests are in tall trees or well-established bushes close to the water's edge; some are in extensive reedbeds. This species is gregarious with other Herons and single nests, or a few pairs, are found in colonies of Little Egret and Night Heron.
Nest untidily arranged sticks and branches, or broken reeds and sedge; no lining material added.
Eggs 4–6, rarely 7; opaque greenish-blue. Size 38·4 × 28·6 mm. Weight 16 g. Incubation 22–24 days. Single brood, mid-May–late June.
Nestlings white and brownish-buff down. Remain in nest for about 32 days.

Bittern* *Botaurus stellaris*
Pl. **240**

Site in dense cover of reeds or rank vegetation on swampy ground such as fenland in Br. Is. Last year's growth of reed or sedge is broken down to form a raft type of nest, anchored by the roots but apparently floating in knee-deep water.
Nest loosely arranged layers of broken stems (reed, etc.), smoothed into a depression in the centre. Diameter about 35 cm, inner depression 5–10 cm, the whole heap 15 cm high.

Some nests are in open water on exposed tussocks, but the majority are hidden by extensive reed cover.
Eggs occasionally 4, generally 5–6; matt olive-brown. Size 52·3 × 38·7 mm. Weight around 40 g. Incubation 25–26 days. One male may pair with two or more females. Single brood, March/April–May/June. Replacement clutch.
Nestlings down reddish on upperparts, pale on underparts; sparse at first, revealing bare patches of skin. Remain in or near nest for 4–5 weeks.

Little Bittern *Ixobrychus minutus*
Pl. **26**

Site usually in dense reedbeds near small pools or more extensive sheets of water, often 20–50 cm above the water; also recorded in trees or bushes in swamps, particularly associated with willows, nightshade and nettles. (Suspected sporadic breeding in East Anglia.)
Nest same type as Bittern but shallower in the centre (about 2–3 cm deep).
Eggs 5–6, occasionally 4 or 7; matt white, chalky surface. Size 34·7 × 26·5 mm. Weight 10–14 g. Incubation 16–19 days. Usually one brood, sometimes two, late May–early July. Replacement clutch.
Nestlings down less sparse than previous species, but some bare patches on head and neck; upperparts reddish-buff, underparts whitish. Remain in nest for about 25–27 days.

STORKS   *Ciconiidae*

Solitary nests in tall trees (Black Stork), groups of nests in trees or on tall buildings (White Stork); large and bulky structures, made out of sticks with a shallow depression in the centre. There are usually 3–5 very large white eggs. One brood per year. Two species breed in central Europe; Black Stork has never bred in Br. Is. and the last record of a pair of White Storks was in Edinburgh in the fifteenth century.

White Stork *Ciconia ciconia*
(Not illustrated)

Site on roofs of houses and farm buildings, particularly when encouraged by presence of old cartwheels already fixed in position to provide a suitable base for the nest. Less frequently in tall trees (oak, alder, poplar, lime) and in pollard willows.

Nest layers of sticks, branches and twigs are plastered with lumps of earth and dirt, making a very bulky structure. (A cartwheel is covered completely.) The depression in the centre is comparatively shallow, lined with leaves, grass, moss, feathers and various bits of local litter. Nests in trees are usually about 75–80 cm wide and about 35 cm high. Nests which are occupied year after year achieve even larger proportions, as much as 1·70 m wide and 1·50–1·90 m high.

Eggs 3–5; chalky-white layer over green or greenish-yellow shell (ground colour shows faintly). Size 71·3 × 51·5 mm. Weight varies around 115 g. Incubation 31–32, sometimes 33 days. Single brood, mid-April–early May. Replacement clutch.

Nestlings white down; blackish bill and feet. Remain in nest for 54–55 days.

Black Stork *Ciconia nigra*
(Not illustrated)

Site in tall trees growing on swampy ground, associated particularly with old forests of mixed species (oak, beech, birch, pine). Nests are mostly 10–15 m from the ground, sometimes higher, built in a fork near the trunk. Cliff-faces are used regularly in southern Europe, seldom in central Europe.

Nest similar to White Stork but smaller and shallower. New nests are about 50 cm wide and 20–25 cm high. Old nests seldom reach such large proportions as in the previous species.

Eggs generally 3–5, sometimes 2, rarely 6, similar to White Stork but colour of shell, under chalky-white layer, shows through as a stronger green. Size 65·3 × 48·8 mm. Weight 86 g. Incubation 30 days. Single brood, May. Replacement clutch (only 3 eggs according to Ray).

Nestlings down white; bill yellow at first, turning whitish. Remain in nest for 62–65 days.

Colonies are associated with reedbeds, freshwater lagoons and marshy ground. Nests are often towards the edge of the reedbed and in some localities they are in trees or bushes, always near open water. The eggs are matt white ground colour, irregularly marked with reddish-brown flecks. Clutch-size usually 3–5. One brood per year. In Europe the main breeding areas are in Holland and Austria; last known record of breeding in Britain was in seventeenth century in East Anglia and, as pairs visit regularly, definite breeding may be recorded again soon.

Spoonbill *Platalea leucorodia*
(Not illustrated)

Site usually 30–40 cm above the water, sometimes up to 60 cm, in extensive reedbeds or low branches of bushes or trees on marshy ground near open water. (Last breeding record seventeenth century in East Anglia.)

Nest platform type of broken reeds and sedge, or sticks and dead twigs in bushes and trees. Shallow inner depression may or may not be lined with grass, tattered paper or feathers. Nests about 80–100 cm wide and about 28 cm high.

Eggs 3–5, exceptionally 6 or 7; matt white ground colour scattered with reddish-brown flecks. Size 67·5 × 45·8 mm. Weight 76 g. Incubation 21–24, sometimes 25 days. Single brood, April–June. Replacement clutch. *Nestlings* whitish down. Leave nest after about 28–32 days.

SWANS, GEESE AND DUCKS *Anatidae*

This family includes Swans, Geese, Ducks (dabbling and diving), Shelducks and Sawbills. Their nests are mostly in vegetation along the banks of quiet stretches of water although some are quite a distance from the water's edge. Other sites include holes in trees (Goldeneye and Goosander) and underground burrows (Shelduck). The majority of nests are well-hidden among vegetation, built of reeds and so on, and lined with down. The eggs have no markings and are of various shades: greyish-green (Mute Swan), creamy-white (Grey Lag and Canada Goose), greenish to bluish-grey or creamy-white (Ducks), creamy-white to buff-olive (Sawbills). Clutches that are complete give some indication, according to the number of eggs present, towards identification: 5–8 (Mute Swan, Grey Lag and Canada Goose); 6–9 or 11 (Pochard, Red-crested Pochard, Goldeneye, Common Scoter); 7–8, 11 or 12 (Wigeon, Mallard, Pintail, Ferruginous Duck, Scaup, Red-breasted Merganser); 8–12 (Shelduck, Gadwall, Teal, Garganey, Shoveler, Tufted Duck, Goosander); 4–6 (Eider). All species are single-brooded, but replacement clutches are common. Of the ducks listed: Scaup do not breed in central Europe; in Br. Is., Red-crested

Pochard only breeds as an 'escape' from ornamental wildfowl collections and Ferruginous Duck does not breed. (Whooper Swan *Cygnus cygnus* is not listed below but breeds sporadically in north Scotland.)

Mute Swan* *Cygnus olor*
Pl. **15**
Site islets in lakes, reedbeds and marshes; preferably near quiet stretches of open water but this species has adapted well to nesting in close proximity to human activities.
Nest huge mound of sticks, reeds and other local vegetation. Size of mound tends to make it conspicuous: about 1·75 m wide and about 30 cm high; depression in the centre (lined with finer material and feathers) about 43 cm across and about 11 cm deep.
Eggs 5–8, sometimes 9; greyish-green, with chalky deposit which gets stained and polished yellowish-brown during incubation. Size 115·0 × 74·1 mm. Weight about 332 g. Incubation 35–36, occasionally 38 days. Single brood, March/April–June. Replacement clutch.
Nestlings greyish-brown down. Leave nest after a day or two; adults sometimes carry them, nestling among the feathers, on their backs while swimming.

Grey Lag Goose* *Anser anser*
(Not illustrated)
Site heather moors and islets in lochs (Scotland); extensive reedbeds, marshes and among brambles in secluded underwood (central Europe).
Nest loose structure of stems or twigs of local plants, including

'platforms' of reeds surrounded by water; depression in centre lined with finer material and down. Diameter about 86 cm, height 22 cm. The depression for the eggs is about 9 cm deep and 25 cm across.
Eggs usually 5–8, sometimes 4 or 9; creamy-white, matt surface which is liable to become stained. Size 85·3 × 58·0 mm. Weight 176 g. Incubation 28–29 days. Single brood, late March–mid-April on the Continent, April–June in Scotland. Replacement clutch.
Nestlings greenish-yellow down with dark greyish-brown markings on head, shoulder and back. Leave nest shortly after hatching.

Canada Goose* *Branta canadensis*
(Not illustrated)
Site islets in lakes and marshy places in vicinity of water; several pairs may nest in the same area, often in the shelter of bushes. This species is adaptable and in Br. Is. it breeds on islets in ornamental lakes and disused gravelpits, also in parks and woodland.
Nest similar to Grey Lag. Depression in centre lined with leaves, grass and greyish-brown down.
Eggs 5–6, sometimes 4 or 11; creamy-white. Size 85·7 × 58·2 mm. Weight 228 g. Incubation 28–30 days. Single brood, March

to May/June. Replacement clutch only when eggs are lost during the initial laying period.

Nestlings greenish-brown down on upperparts, yellower on underparts. Leave nest shortly after hatching.

Shelduck* *Tadorna tadorna*
Pl. **22**

Site usually in sandy burrow, occasionally above ground, water in the vicinity; often on estuary marshes or in dunes near the sea. Rabbit burrows frequently used, occasionally badger's sett or fox's earth. Sites above ground are usually in sheltered position, under a bush or in a hollow tree.

Nest simple scrape, lined with pale grey down, often several feet from entrance of burrow. Withered vegetation mixed with a mass of down in nests above ground.

Eggs sometimes 7, usually 8–12; creamy-white, slightly glossy. Size 65·8 × 47·6 mm. Weight 78 g. Incubation 28–29, occasionally 30 days. Single brood, April/May–June/July. Replacement clutch.

Nestlings down on upperparts white and dark brown, yellowish-white on underparts, chest-band does not show until later. Leave nest shortly after hatching, able to fly at about 8 weeks.

Mallard* *Anas platyrhynchos*
Pl. **17**

Site usually on the ground near water in thick ground cover or a few feet up in branches overhanging riverbank; also by small pools in woodland, in tree-stumps and pollard willows. Sometimes takes over old nests of other species high up in trees; also nests on buildings in urban areas. Much more adaptable than other Duck species.

Nest bulky structure of leaves, stems and grass, with a few feathers and lots of greyish-brown down in the centre.

Eggs 7–11, but sometimes 5 or up to 16; greenish colour but very variable (blue-green, buff-green, grey-green), with a waxy surface. Size 58·4 × 39·5 mm. Weight 49–50 g. Incubation 28 days, but, according to Bauer-Glutz, varies between 24–32 days. Single brood, peak period March–May but nests recorded from February to November. Replacement clutch.

Nestlings olive-brown down with patches of pale yellow. Leave nest shortly after hatching.

Gadwall* *Anas strepera*
(Not illustrated)

Site in thickets of reeds or other vegetation near open stretches of water, often along the banks under overhanging branches of bushes; also on islets in lakes where there is less ground cover. This species favours dry ground close to water.

Nest similar to Mallard but looks more neatly constructed, and the down lining is a darker brown.

Eggs 8–12, sometimes 6 or 13; creamy-buff. Size 51·8 × 37·5 mm. Weight 42·3 (39·7–43·5) g. Incubation 26 days. Single brood,

May–June. Replacement clutch. *Nestlings* similar to Mallard but the bill is pale brown. Leave nest shortly after hatching.

Teal* *Anas crecca*
(Not illustrated)

Site nearly always well-hidden in vegetation on dry ground, usually along water ditches or by small pools but also recorded some distance from water. Sites include bracken in woodland and heather on moors.

Nest bits of local plants with a rounded depression in the centre, lined with spotted down.

Eggs 5, sometimes 8–10; pale creamy-buff with a greenish tinge. Size 45·6 × 33·5 mm. Weight 26·8. Incubation 21–22, occasionally 23 days. Single brood, April–June. Replacement clutch.

Nestlings dark grey down with rufous tinge on upperparts, yellowish-white on underparts. Leave nest shortly after hatching.

Garganey* *Anas querquedula*
Pl. **18**

Site similar to Teal, favours secluded stretches of water sheltered by sedge and similar vegetation. Nests in meadows as well as on marshes and moorland.

Nest similar to Teal, lined with white-tipped down.

Eggs 8–11, sometimes 6 or up to 14; creamy-buff without any greenish tinge. Size 45·3 × 33·3 mm. Weight 22·8–28·6 g. Incubation 21–23 days. Single brood, April–June. Replacement clutch.

Nestlings very similar to Mallard except for two dark stripes on side of head. Leave nest shortly after hatching.

Wigeon* *Anas penelope*
(Not illustrated)

Site on islets or along the banks of lochs hidden in thick cover (including heather), between tree-roots or under branches overhanging the edge of the water. Favours sites close to water but also found some distance away.

Nest dry bits of local plants, lined with ashen-grey down; distinguished from Gadwall's nest with difficulty, except when helped by presence of typical white contour feathers.

Eggs 9, sometimes 7–8, exceptionally 10; creamy-buff, occasionally with a bluish tinge. Size 53·9 × 38·2 mm. Weight 44 g. Incubation 22–23, less frequently 24 days. Single brood, April–June. Replacement clutch.

Nestlings darker brown down (with cinnamon-buff patches) than Mallard; eye-stripe well defined and sometimes a darker streak from lores to below the eye; underparts creamy-buff. Leave nest shortly after hatching.

Pintail* *Anas acuta*
Pl. **19**

Site favours extensive moors and marshes where vegetation is comparatively short. Some nests are right out in the open, others hidden by grass undergrowth. Nearly always in a hollow on dry ground and not necessarily close to water.

Nest dry bits of local plants

arranged carelessly in a depression on the ground, similar construction to Mallard, lined with grass and down (grey and brown).

Eggs 7–11, occasionally 5 or 12; yellowish-green to creamy-buff. Size 51·8 × 37·0 mm. Weight 47 g. Incubation 22–23 days. Single brood, April–May in the south, May–June in the north. Replacement clutch.

Nestlings greyish-brown down with light patches, some white on the head. Leave nest shortly after hatching.

Shoveler* *Anas clypeata*
Pl. **20**

Site favour marshes with small pools, particularly where rank vegetation provides adequate cover. (Long grass growing up through a thorn-bush sometimes conceals the nest.) Also in meadows and on dry heath or moorland, not necessarily close to water.

Nest hidden in hollow or under a bush, made out of local plants and lined with grass. Down in central depression is ashen-grey with pale centre.

Eggs generally 8–12, sometimes 7; greenish-grey, occasionally yellowish. Size 51·8 × 37·0 mm. Weight 39 (35–43) g. Incubation 23–25 days. Single brood, April/May–June. Replacement clutch.

Nestlings greyish-yellow down with paler patches along the flanks; dark grey bill does not develop characteristic spatulate shape until later. Leave nest shortly after hatching.

Red-crested Pochard* *Netta rufina*
(Not illustrated)

Site reedbeds or similar dense cover near water where disturbance is unlikely. Nest often on raised site (such as broken stems of sedge, tussocks of rush, grassy hummock on islet), and always well-hidden. (British breeding records probably 'escapes' from ornamental wildfowl collections.)

Nest pile of local aquatic plants, hollowed out in centre, sometimes neatly arranged and conspicuously built-up; lined with grass, leaves, finer stems and brownish down.

Eggs 6–12; pale yellowish-grey, matt surface. Nests containing a large number of eggs, 16–24, represent clutches laid by more than one female. Size 58·2 × 42·0 mm. Weight 50 g. Incubation about 26 days. Single brood, late May–June. Replacement clutch.

Nestlings down on upperparts olive-brown with pale patches, yellowish-white on underparts. Leave nest shortly after hatching.

Pochard* *Aythya ferina*
(Not illustrated)

Site on the edges of pools and lakes in dense cover of reeds, flags, rushes, etc., or under briars and branches along the banks, nearly always very close to water.

Nest made out of local plants, the heap of nesting material may be quite substantial in shallow water, depression in the centre lined with grass, leaves and down (dark brown with pale centre). *Eggs* sometimes 4, usually 6–9; greenish or yellowish-grey, acquire a polished look during incubation. Size 61·3 × 43·7 mm. Weight 66–68 g. Incubation 24–26, occasionally 28 days. Single brood, mid-April–June/July. Replacement clutch.

Nestlings dark brown and greenish-yellow down. Leave nest shortly after hatching.

Ferruginous Duck *Aythya nyroca*
Pl. **16, 239**

Site close to water in marshes and swamps, hidden in vegetation or anchored on submerged bank of dead sedge, etc. in shallow water.

Nest similar to Pochard, broken stems of local plants with a depression in the centre, lined with bits of local plants and down (dark brown with pale centre and also pale at the top).

Eggs 7–11, sometimes 5 or 12, short ovate; warm buff or yellowish-brown. Size 52·1 × 37·9 mm. Weight 43 g. Incubation 25–27, occasionally 28 days. Single brood, mid-May–mid-June. Replacement clutch.

Nestlings dark brown upperparts with indistinct pale mottling, yellowish underparts. Leave nest shortly after hatching.

Scaup* *Aythya marila*
(Not illustrated)

Site on islands in comparatively deep lakes (mainly in Scotland), also on northern moors and tundra. Several pairs often breed in the same area; some nests are on open ground, others among hummocks of heather or tussocks of rough grass. (This species does not breed in central Europe.)

Nest on dry sites there may be nothing except bits of local plants and down lining the hollow; the down is reminiscent of Pochard. On damp sites the mound of nesting material may be built up to a height of about 15 cm and 28 cm wide.

Eggs 7–11, occasionally 6 or 13; matt greenish-grey, difficult to distinguish from Tufted Duck. Nests containing many eggs, 17–22, represent clutches laid by more than one female. Size 63·2 × 43·5 mm. Weight 60 g. Incubation 24–25, occasionally 26 days. Single brood, May–June· Replacement clutch.

Nestlings olive-brown and greenish-yellow down, similar to Tufted Duck. Leave nest shortly after hatching.

Tufted Duck* *Aythya fuligula*
(Not illustrated)

Site on islets and banks of lakes, in thick cover, either in very boggy ground or surrounded by water. Favours tall grass or reeds which form a 'tent' over the nest-hollow. There may be several pairs nesting in same area.

Nest looks much greener than other Ducks' nests because the hollow is lined with plenty of grass and only a little down (dark brown and reminiscent of Pochard).

Eggs sometimes 5, usually 8–11; greenish-grey. Size 59·9 × 41·3 mm. Weight 55·7 g. Incubation 23–25 days. Single brood, May/

June–July/August. Replacement clutch.

Nestlings various dark streaks over the eye; olive-brown upperparts, pale underparts. Leave nest shortly after hatching.

Goldeneye* *Bucephala clangula*
(Not illustrated)

Site natural holes or old woodpecker-holes in tree-trunks or branches; also recorded in rabbit burrows, rock crevices and nestboxes. Favours wooded country near lakes and rivers. On the Continent many occupied holes are found in trees on stabilized sand-dunes; the majority of occupied sites are at a height of 3–5 m, some even higher, in trees. (In Br. Is. probably confined to Scotland.)

Nest no material, the decaying wood often has a layer of humus in the hole. Pale bluish-grey down is not added until the clutch is complete.

Eggs 6–11, short ovate; bluishgreen. Size 58·4 × 43·2 mm. Weight 55–58 g. Incubation 30, although sometimes 29 days. Single brood, mid-April—May. Replacement clutch.

Nestlings black and white down, dark upperparts with two white patches, white underparts. Clamber out of nest-hole, apparently tumbling to the ground or into the water 1 to 2 days after hatching.

Common Scoter* *Melanitta nigra*
(Not illustrated)

Site northern moorland or tundra broken up by lochans and small pools. Nests are among heather, rough grass or dwarf scrub, and usually near water. (In Br. Is. confined to Scotland and N.W. Ireland.)

Nest a hollow in the shelter of low vegetation, decorated with bits of grass, moss or lichen. Feathers and down are mixed with the lining material. (Feathers are grey with a pale tip; down is brown with a pale centre.)

Eggs 6–9, sometimes 10; colour varies from pale creamy buff to dark buff or brown. Size 65·6 × 44·6 mm. Weight 63–74 g. Incubation 30–31 days. Single brood, May–June or early July in northern areas. Replacement clutch.

Nestlings brownish-black down on upperparts, greyish-white on underparts. Leave nest shortly after hatching.

Eider* *Somateria mollissima*
Pl. **21**

Site usually near the sea but sometimes on islets in freshwater (lakes and rivers) some distance from the coast. Colonies vary in size. Inaccessible islands often have large colonies. Nests are frequently found in comparatively open sites and between rocks or near driftwood and seaweed, but also in rough grass or heather. (Confined to northern areas in Br. Is.)

Nest a depression decorated with bits of local material and the typical soft down of this species (greyish-brown with lighter patches). The nest is usually about

17 cm wide and 6–7 cm deep. *Eggs* 4–6, sometimes 3 or 7–8; glossy greenish-grey to buff-olive. Nests with 8 eggs or more represent clutches laid by more than one female. Size 77·6 × 51·9 mm. Weight 110·3 g. Incubation 25–26, occasionally 27 days. Single brood, April/May–July. Replacement clutch.

Nestlings pale eye-stripe; blackish-grey and brownish-white down. Leave nest shortly after hatching.

Red-breasted Merganser*
Mergus serrator
Pl. **245**

Site on the coast near the sea or inland near freshwater, hidden in some kind of cover on dry ground on moors, marshes and dunes. Shelter for the nest may be provided by tree-roots, rocks or hummocks of heather and rough grass. Also recorded under sheds and heaps of brushwood near human habitation. (Confined to northern areas in Br. Is.)

Nest a hollow with an accumulation of leaves, grass and bits of local plants, lined with greyish-brown down.

Eggs usually 7–12, more rarely 5–14; matt surface, buff-olive (darker than Goosander). Size 65·6 × 45·1 mm. Weight about 75 g. Incubation 28–32 days. Single brood May–July. Replacement clutch.

Nestlings brownish down on upperparts with three white patches above the wing, white underparts. Leave nest shortly after hatching.

Goosander* *Mergus merganser*
Pl. **246**

Site differs from Red-breasted Merganser. Majority of nests are at a height of 10–18 m above ground, sometimes lower (1–8 m) in natural holes of trees (willow, oak, beech, poplar). Occupied nest-holes are usually near water but not invariably and holes in walls, or crevices in cliffs, may be used when tree-holes are not available. Nests have also been recorded at ground level between tree-roots by the water's edge. (In Britain confined to northern areas.)

Nest no material in tree-holes other than humus or rotting wood. More exposed nests are lined with leaves, grass, lichen and other plant material. The down is whitish-grey and the female normally covers the eggs with it before leaving the nest.

Eggs 8–12, occasionally 6; matt surface, creamy-white (lighter than Red-breasted Merganser). Size 66·4 × 46·4 mm. Weight 83–84 g. Incubation 32, sometimes 35 days. Single brood, April–May/June. Replacement clutch.

Nestlings dark brown down on upperparts with two white patches above the wing, white underparts. Clamber out of nest-hole, apparently tumbling to the ground or into the water a day or two after hatching.

VULTURES   *Aegypiidae*

Nests are rudimentary, often only a few sticks, in a tall tree or crevice in steep cliff. Old nests of other species (Eagles, etc.) may be taken over. A number of pairs may build close together but solitary nests also occur. Normally there is only one egg, white without markings of any kind, and only one clutch per year. One species breeds in southern Europe.

Griffon Vulture *Gyps fulvus*
(Not illustrated)

Site rock crevices of steep cliffs or in tall trees; sometimes uses old nests of other species. Solitary or sociable in both sites.

Nest a few sticks and a few feathers.

Egg 1; white, unmarked. Size 92·0 × 70·1 mm. Weight 252 g. Incubation 48–50 days. Single brood, February–March.

Nestling remains in nest for about 3 months.

BIRDS OF PREY (ACCIPITERS)   *Accipitridae*

This family includes Hawks, Eagles, Buzzards, Kites and Harriers. Except for the Harriers, which are ground-nesters, all nest at a considerable height either on cliff-faces or in tall trees, and build a foundation of sticks and branches. This foundation may be bulky or less substantial and may be decorated or lined with fresh greenery (Hawks, Eagles, Buzzards), bits of paper and clods of earth or dung (Kites), or with grass (Harriers). The eggs are whitish, some have dark stains or flecks; hair-line marks are typical of kites. Clutch-size is mostly 2–4 or 5. There is one brood per year. Fifteen species breed in central Europe, of which 10 also breed in Br. Is.

Goshawk* *Accipiter gentilis*
Pl. **56**

Site mature trees (beech, oak, spruce, pine), usually close to the trunk and at a considerable height (16–22 m). Favours an old tree which stands on its own rather than a dense forest. Old nests of other species, such as Kites and Buzzards, are sometimes taken over.

Nest bulky foundation of sticks and branches, 1 m wide and 50 cm high; central depression 6–10 cm deep, lined with leaves.

Fresh green branches are added during incubation period.

Eggs 3–4, sometimes 5; greenish-white, usually unmarked but soon become stained and sometimes there are rust or purplish-grey markings. Size 56·6 × 42·7 mm. Weight about 60 g. Incubation sometimes 36, usually 38 days. Single brood, April–May/June.

Nestlings whitish down; greyish-black iris which becomes paler; pink feet which become yellow. Leave nest after 36–40 days.

Sparrowhawk* *Accipiter nisus*
Pl. **57**
Site both deciduous and ever-green trees, usually close to the trunk (5–10 m above ground) but also recorded in low bushes. Favours a conifer in mixed wood-land towards the edge of a ride or by a river running through forest. Old nests of other species are also used (Jay, Crow, Wood Pigeon, squirrel's drey, etc.).
Nest bulky, untidy structure like a large version of a Pigeon's nest. Bits of bark, twigs, spruce needles or leaves form a lining. As the female moults at this time some nests are full of feathers (see illustration). Width about 20 cm, central depression about 6 cm deep.
Eggs 4–6, short ovate; bluish-white with lots of purplish-grey and dark brown flecks; markings tend to be concentrated at blunt end. Size 39·8 × 31·8 mm. Weight 20–22 g. Incubation sometimes 31, usually 33 days. Single brood, May–June.
Nestlings white down is short and dense. Leave nest after 26–30 days.

Osprey* *Pandion haliaetus*
Pl. **244**
Site always in vicinity of water. High up in crown of tall tree (favours pine and spruce in Scotland) or on cliff-face over-looking the sea; also recorded on the ground among rocks or shingle on the shore.
Nest bulky foundation of sticks and branches, lined with rotting bark and other local plant material (heather, moss, etc.). *Eggs* 3–4, sometimes 5; chalky-white, marked with reddish-brown and grey blotches. Size 61·6 × 46·4 mm. Weight about 68–71 g. Incubation occasionally 35, usually 37–38 days. Single brood, April–May/June. Re-placement clutch has been re-corded.
Nestlings very sparse down at first, sandy and greyish-brown later which makes them look speckled. Able to fly after 57–60, more rarely 63 days.

Golden Eagle* *Aquila chrysaetos*
(Not illustrated)
Site ledges on steep rock-face (usually inaccessible), also in mature trees and occasionally on the ground; in remote highlands or mountains.
Nest substantial structure of branches and clods of earth, decorated with greenery (such as woodrush), and there is often a lot of dead grass in the central depression. Some nest-sites are occupied again and again over the years; a pair may have two or three traditional sites, using each one in turn. Nests may be 2–3 m wide and 1·50–2 m high.
Eggs 2, sometimes 3; white, some are dead white, others have various blotches and flecks (red-dish or grey) which tend to be concentrated at one end. Size 77·0 × 59·5 mm. Weight 140 g. Incubation 42–44 days. Single brood, March/April–May/June. Replacement clutch has been recorded.
Nestlings greyish-whitish down,

becoming creamy white later. Fed in nest for 75–80 days.

Lesser Spotted Eagle *Aquila pomarina*
(Not illustrated)

Site at varying heights in tall trees, usually in birch, oak or beech but also recorded in spruce. Favours isolated trees along the edges of rides with water in the vicinity.

Nest uses old nests of other species (Goshawk, Buzzard) or builds a new foundation of branches and sticks, lining it with fresh grass and greenery from broad-leaved or evergreen trees. *Eggs* 2, sometimes 1; dull white with various markings (light brown, reddish-brown, purplish-grey). Size 62·9 × 50·6 mm. Weight around 83 g. Incubation 42–44 days. Single brood, mid-May.

Nestlings greyish-white down; feathered feet. Remain in nest for 7–8 weeks.

Booted Eagle *Hieraaetus pennatus*
(Not illustrated)

Site high up in tall trees, deciduous and evergreen, often near a ride or clearing in the forest. Also on inaccessible rock-faces.

Nest bulky foundation of branches, lined with green leaves.

Eggs 2; white, usually unmarked but occasionally a few reddish-brown flecks. Size 55·0 × 44·2 mm. Weight 62 g. Incubation about 35 days. Single brood, May.

Nestlings remain in nest for 47–50, sometimes 52 days.

Buzzard* *Buteo buteo*
Pl. **55**

Site tall trees, deciduous and evergreen, often in the fork of a tree growing on outskirts of wood or copse at a height 8–15, occasionally 20 m from the ground. Also on rocky ledges of sea-cliffs.

Nest usually about 72 cm wide, made out of branches, bracken, heather or similar coarse material, lined with bits of bark, moss, and leaves; fresh greenery is added from time to time.

Eggs 2–3, less often 4; dull white with variable amount of markings (reddish-brown and purplish-grey). Some are uniform white. Size 56·0 × 44·7 mm. Weight about 61 g. Incubation sometimes 31, generally 34–36 days. Single brood, April–May/June.

Nestlings sparse down (greyish and white) revealing bare patches of pink skin. Leave nest after 6–7 weeks.

Honey Buzzard* *Pernis apivorus*
Pl. **243**

Site high up in tall deciduous trees (oak, alder) towards the edge of a wood or near a clearing.

Nest old nests of other species (Buzzard, Goshawk) may be used or a new foundation built out of branches; width 80–100 cm, height about 40 cm and depression 5, occasionally 6, cm deep. The depression is lined with leaves or sprays of greenery from oak, beech or lime trees.

Eggs 2; yellowish-white ground colour but so heavily marked that they look as though they were colour-washed a reddish-brown. Size 50·8 × 41·1 mm. Weight about 53 g. Incubation 33–34 days. Single brood, late May–early June/July. Replacement clutch.

Nestlings greyish-white down, becoming whiter; pinkish feet. Remain in nest for 40–45, more rarely 46 days.

Short-toed Eagle *Circaetus gallicus*
(Not illustrated)

Site tall trees on remote hillsides or mountain gorges and near open stretches of marsh or moor. A tree growing near a quiet glade or clearing is usually selected.

Nest similar to Buzzard, foundation of branches with fresh greenery added during incubation period.

Egg 1; chalky white, unmarked. Size 75·8 × 60·4 mm. Weight 174 g. Incubation around 40 days.

Nestling remains in nest for about 75 days.

Red Kite* *Milvus milvus*
Pl. **241**

Site high up in the crown, or on a stout branch, of mature trees (beech, oak, spruce, pine), usually near a clearing or towards the outskirts of plantation.

Nest uses old nests of other species (Buzzard, occasionally Crow) or builds a new foundation out of branches. Width at least 80–100 cm. The shallow depression for the eggs contains various bits of rubbish as well as grass, roots, clods of earth and dung. Presence of rubbish and carrion is typical of Kite's nest.

Eggs 2–4; dull white ground colour with reddish-brown flecks and typical hair-line markings. Some eggs are difficult to distinguish from Buzzard. Size 56·6 × 44·6 mm. Weight varies around 54 g. Incubation 28–30, occasionally 32 days. Single brood, April–May. Replacement clutch.

Nestlings rufous-buff or buff down, becoming paler later; brownish-grey iris. Remain in nest for 48–50, rarely 54 days.

Black Kite *Milvus migrans*
Pl. **242**

Site favours tall spruce or pine in the vicinity of water but also recorded in oak and alder trees; majority of nests are at a height of 8–15 m, some at 20–25 m. Old nests of other species (Crow, Buzzard, Heron) are also used. (Last bred in Britain probably Middle Ages.)

Nest fresh branches may be added to old nest of other species or an entirely new nest made out of branches; lining material consists of clods of earth, paper, rags, sheep's wool and moss. Dimensions similar to Red Kite: width 80–100 cm, inner depression about 6 cm deep.

Eggs 2, sometimes 3, occasionally 4; chalky white ground colour with a few reddish-brown flecks and typical hair-line markings. Size 56·6 × 44·6 mm. Weight varies around 55 g. Incubation generally 29–30 days, sometimes

28. Single brood, late April–May. Replacement clutch.
Nestlings yellowish-white down, becoming darker later (grey-brown). Pink feet. Remain in nest for 42–45 days.

White-tailed Eagle *Haliaeetus albicilla*
(Not illustrated)

Site rocky ledges of cliff-faces and large trees (cork, beech, spruce). Ground nests are found in steppe country but most tree-nests are at a height of 15–20 m above ground. (Last breeding records in Br. Is. early this century.)
Nest bulky foundation of branches, decorated with greenery around the edges and lined with grass, lichen and moss. Same site may be used over several years and nests often reach huge dimensions, sometimes 180–220 cm wide and 1 m high.
Eggs 2, occasionally 3; chalky white with yellow stain-marks. Size 72·3 × 56·1 mm. Weight around 140 g. Incubation 35, although sometimes 34 or 40 days. Single brood, late February–April. Replacement clutch.
Nestlings whitish down, becoming buff-grey later. Dark iris and bill. Remain in nest for 10–11, occasionally 12 weeks.

Marsh Harrier* *Circus aeruginosus*
Pl. **59**

Site marshes and fenland (mainly confined to East Anglia), hidden in extensive reedbeds on swampy ground in shallow water; similar sites on the Continent.

Nest reeds and sedge form a bulky pile which varies in height (often 40–50 cm). Grasses are used to line the nest.
Eggs 4–5, sometimes 6; chalky-white, nearly always without any well-defined marking but soon become stained. Size 49·2 × 38·1 mm. Weight 40 g. Incubation 33–36 days. Single brood, April/May–June/July. Replacement clutch.
Nestlings short down, buff and white; dark eye-stripe develops later. Remain in nest for 34–36, less often 38 days.

Hen Harrier* *Circus cyaneus*
(Not illustrated)

Site on damp ground, usually among heather or rank vegetation of moors and marshes; in a few areas in northern half of Br. Is. On the Continent, also recorded in damp fields of root-crops and young conifer plantations.
Nest dead stems of heather, bracken and other local material packed down into a hollow, hidden in some kind of ground cover, and lined with grass.
Eggs 4–5, more rarely 6; chalky white, usually unmarked but often become stained and some have a few well-defined markings (brownish-grey). Size 45·2 × 35·6 mm. Weight 30 g. Incubation occasionally 29, usually 30–32 days. Single brood, April/May–June. Replacement clutch.
Nestlings white down, becoming greyer later. Remain in nest for 32–34 days.

Montagu's Harrier* *Circus pygargus*
Pl. **60, 232**

Site damp marshes, dry heathland and dunes, also among young plantations where ground cover is adequate; now in very few areas of Br. Is. On the Continent, nests are also found among field crops.

Nest foundation of twigs and coarse stems, lined with finer material and grass.

Eggs 3–5; white or bluish-white, without any well-defined markings but occasionally with mud-coloured stains. Size 41·5 × 32·6 mm. Weight around 25 g. Incubation generally 29–30, less often 28, days. Single brood, May–July.

Nestlings white down. Remain in nest for about 35 days.

FALCONS   *Falconidae*

Falcons do not build a proper nest for themselves. The eggs are either laid in old nests of other species (members of the Crow family or other Birds of Prey) or directly in a rock crevice or on a ledge of some kind. Sites include trees, buildings, cliffs and open country with low ground cover. The eggs are heavily marked (reddish-brown) on whitish ground colour. Usually 3–5 eggs in a clutch; one brood per year. Four species breed both in central Europe and Br. Is.

Kestrel* *Falco tinnunculus*
Pl. **58**

Site ledges and crevices of tall buildings and steep cliffs, also old nests of other species (Carrion Crow, Magpie, Buzzard) which build in trees. Height from the ground is usually 8–12 m.

Nest no material used to construct a nest. Old nests are flattened, eggs are laid in a mere scrape.

Eggs 5–6, occasionally 7; yellowish-white ground colour often so heavily marked with reddish-brown that no white is visible. Size 39·3 × 31·3 mm. Weight about 21 g. Incubation 28–30, sometimes 31, days. Single brood, April–May/June.

Nestlings white down, short and dense. Remain in nest for 27–33 days.

Hobby* *Falco subbuteo*
Pl. **228**

Site old nests of other species (Carrion Crow, Magpie, Buzzard), particularly when these are in trees towards the edge of a wood or scattered in open country. Height from the ground is usually 15–20 m.

Nest no material used to construct a nest. Old nests are flattened.

Eggs 3, less often 4; yellowish-white ground colour is almost obliterated by reddish-brown or lighter brown stippling. Size 41·6 × 32·7 mm. Weight around 24 g. Incubation 28 days. Single brood, May–June/July.

Nestlings short white down. Pink bill and feet. Remain in nest for 28–32 days.

Merlin* *Falco columbarius*
Pl. **229**

Site usually on the ground among heather or rough grass on moors or hill pastures; also on sand-dunes and tundra. Occasionally takes over old nest of other species (Crow family) in a tree standing in open country.
Nest bits of vegetation flattened into a scrape which may be lined with bents and lichen or moss.
Eggs 4–6; yellowish-white ground colour is almost obliterated by reddish-brown markings similar to Kestrel. Size 39·9 × 31·3 mm. Weight 21 g. Incubation 25–26 days. Single brood, May–June.
Nestlings white down. Remain in nest for 25, sometimes 26, days.

Peregrine* *Falco peregrinus*
Pl. **231**

Site steep sea-cliffs and inland crags, church spires and tall buildings with ledges or holes in the walls; also in old nests of other species (Crows, Kites and Buzzards), particularly when in a tall conifer standing on its own. (In Br. Is. the Peregrine is now mainly associated with secluded stretches of cliffs.)
Nest no nesting material; eggs are laid in bare crevice or on flattened debris of old nest of other species.
Eggs 3–4, short ovate; yellowish-white ground colour is usually obliterated by reddish-brown markings. Size 53·3 × 42·3 mm. Weight varies around 48 g. Incubation 29–30 days. Single brood, late March/April–June/July.
Nestlings white down. Pink bill. Remain in nest for 35–38, occasionally 40 days.

GROUSE
Tetraonidae

Members of this family make scrapes hidden in low cover or scree which are difficult to spot. Very little lining material is used, a few bits of dry grass, dead leaves and moss; this acts as effective camouflage for the drab-coloured eggs which are covered by the lining material before the nest is left unattended. Markings on the ground colour also help to break up the outline of the eggs.

Key to the eggs: yellowish-grey with reddish-brown flecks running into each other (Capercaillie); yellow-ochre with lots of reddish-brown spots and dark brown flecks (Black Grouse); yellow-ochre with larger, blackish blotches (Ptarmigan); reddish-yellow with a few brown flecks (Hazel Hen); yellow-ochre with strongly marked brownish and black flecks (Willow Grouse). There are usually 6–10 eggs in a clutch, and one brood per year. Five species breed in central Europe; two of these (Hazel Hen and Willow Grouse) do not breed in Br. Is.

Capercaillie* *Tetrao urogallus*
Pl. **51**

Site woodlands in hills, with ground cover under the trees, and open heather moors. Nests are sheltered by scrub or undergrowth (such as juniper, heather, whortleberry) and are often at the foot of a tree (see illustration). Conifer forests tend to be favoured (Scotland).

Nest a scrape lined with bits of dry grass, dead leaves, pine needles and sometimes a few feathers from the adult.

Eggs sometimes 5, usually 6–10, yellowish-grey ground colour with lots of reddish-brown flecks. Size 57·7 × 41·6 mm. Weight around 50 g. Incubation 26–28 days. Single brood, April–June. Replacement clutch.

Nestlings brownish down on upperparts, yellowish underparts; black lines and blotches on the head. Leave nest shortly after hatching.

Black Grouse* *Lyrurus tetrix*
Pl. **50**

Site open moors or lightly wooded uplands with adequate ground cover, similar to Capercaillie. Nests are found up to the tree-line in mountains.

Nest a scrape in the shelter of heather, scrub birch, juniper, etc., lined with bits of local vegetation and sometimes a few feathers from the adults.

Eggs 6–10, occasionally 12; yellow-ochre ground colour speckled with lots of reddish-brown spots and dark brown flecks. Size 50·2 × 36·1 mm.

Weight 33–36 g. Incubation around 26 days. Single brood, April/May—June/July.

Nestlings similar to Capercaillie but slightly darker on upper parts, and chestnut patch on crown is well-defined by black line. Leave nest shortly after hatching.

Hazel Hen *Tetrastes bonasia*
Pl. **223**

Site similar upland habitat to Black Grouse but also recorded locally at lower altitudes. Nests are well-hidden in undergrowth of branches, bracken, scrub, etc.

Nest a scrape with a few dead leaves and feathers from the adult.

Eggs 8–11, sometimes 7 or 12; reddish-yellow ground colour with a few brown flecks. Size 40·8 × 28·9 mm. Weight 20 g. Incubation 21–25 days. Single brood, April–June. Replacement clutch.

Nestlings reddish-brown down and broad, dark eye-stripe. Leave nest shortly after hatching.

Ptarmigan* *Lagopus mutus*
Pl. **52**

Site among scree or under rock overhangs on mountains; usually on comparatively bare ground but also recorded among vegetation in alpine meadows. (In Br. Is. confined to Scotland.)

Nest a scrape, scantily lined with grass and feathers from the adult.

Eggs 6–10, less often 12; yellow-ochre ground colour with large brownish or black blotches. Size

41·2 × 29.9 mm. Weight around 19 g. Incubation 21–24 days. Single brood, May–July/August.

Nestlings marbled pattern of buff and black down on upperparts; whitish patch on throat, yellowish underparts. Leave nest shortly after hatching.

Willow Grouse *Lagopus lagopus*
Pl. **224**

Site moors and heaths with thick undergrowth or scrub, such as juniper, birch and willow. Nests are often on sunny slopes, hidden by ground cover.

Nest a scrape, scantily lined with dry grass, rootlets, moss or lichen.

Eggs 6–10, sometimes 11; yellow-ochre ground colour, heavily marked with brownish and black flecks. Size 42·7 × 30·9 mm. Weight 22 g. Incubation 21–24,

less often 25 days. Single brood, May–June.

Nestlings marbled pattern of light brown, chestnut and black down. Leave nest shortly after hatching.

Red Grouse* *Lagopus lagopus scoticus*
Pl. **226**

Site moors and peat-bogs with typical vegetation of heather, bilberry, crowberry, tussocks of grass and rushes.

Nest a scrape, scantily lined with bits of grass or other local vegetation.

Eggs 6–11, similar to Willow Grouse. Size 41·2 × 29·9 mm. Weight around 22 g. Incubation 24–25 days. Single brood, March –June.

Nestlings similar to Willow Grouse. Leave nest shortly after hatching.

PARTRIDGES AND PHEASANTS   *Phasianidae*

Nests are mere scrapes, scantily lined with bits of grass and leaves, and well-hidden in ground cover.

Key to the eggs: yellowish-brown, lightly marked with a few reddish-brown spots (Red-legged Partridge); brownish-yellow with very dark marbling (Quail); yellowish-white delicately marked with reddish-brown flecks (Rock Partridge); olive-brown to greenish-grey without marking (Partridge); olive-brown to olive-grey without any marking (Pheasant). There are usually 7–14 eggs in a clutch and one brood per year. Five species breed in central Europe; one of these, the Rock Partridge, does not breed in Br. Is. except as an 'escape' from game preserves.

Red-legged Partridge* *Alectoris rufa*
Pl. **48**

Site favours dry ground (sandy or stony soil), cultivated or uncultivated, including heathland,

rough pasture on downs, orchards and vineyards. Nests are well-hidden by ground cover.

Nest a scrape lined with leaves or grass; sometimes there are also a few feathers from the adult.

Eggs 10–15, less commonly 18; yellowish-brown ground colour, scantily marked with reddish or light brown spots. Size 41·4 × 31·0 mm. Weight around 24 g. Incubation 24–26 days. Single brood, April–July. Replacement clutch.

Nestlings marbled pattern of buff and chestnut down. Leave nest shortly after hatching.

Rock Partridge* *Alectoris graeca*
Pl. **225**

Site among scree, under boulders or rock overhangs; also in shelter of plants growing at high altitudes on the Continent, such as alpine rose, juniper and dwarf pine. (In Br. Is. breeds as an 'escape' from game preserves.)

Nest a scrape lined with bits of dry stems, moss and a few feathers of the adult.

Eggs 9–15, although 6–18 are not unknown; yellowish-white ground colour, delicately marked with reddish-brown flecks. Size 41·1 × 30·6 mm. Weight 23–25 g. Incubation about 25 days. Single brood, April–June. According to Berndt-Meise, two nests of eggs are brooded simultaneously, the male sitting on one and the female on the other; Makatsch states that both parents sharing incubation at the same nest has not been established.

Nestlings leave the nest shortly after hatching.

Partridge* *Perdix perdix*
Pl. **46**

Site arable fields, bordered by rough verges or hedgerows, also waste land with brambles and briars or some kind of ground cover which makes the nest difficult to see from above.

Nest a scrape lined with a little dry grass and leaves. During the laying period and before the clutch is complete, the lining material is pulled over the eggs while the nest is left unattended according to Makatsch.

Eggs 10–20, sometimes 22; unmarked, colour varies from olive-brown to greenish-grey. Size 35·5 × 27·0 mm. Weight around 14 g. Incubation 23–25, less commonly 26 days. Single brood, April–July. Replacement clutch.

Nestlings down on upperparts reddish-brown with black blotches and streaks, underparts yellowish-buff. Leave nest shortly after hatching.

Quail* *Coturnix coturnix*
Pl. **47**

Site arable fields, often in standing corn and clover, also favours uncultivated land with tussocks of grass.

Nest a scrape lined with plenty of dry grass.

Eggs 7–14, occasionally 15; brownish-yellow or yellowish-white ground colour and brownish-black markings, giving marbled effect. Size 30·1 × 23·0 mm. Weight 8–9 g. Incubation around 17 days. Single brood, mid-May–June. Later clutches also recorded, July–September; the latter, according to Makatsch, are probably replacement clutches.

Nestlings reddish-brown down on

upperparts, yellowish underparts; two black stripes on head and back. Leave nest shortly after hatching.

Pheasant* *Phasianus colchicus*
Pl. **49**
Site hedge-bottoms and rough verges of cultivated fields, underwoods and young plantations with patches of bracken and bramble (usually towards the edge of woodland), parkland and large gardens; nests are nearly always on the ground in some kind of low cover.

Nest a scrape lined with a little dry grass and dead leaves.
Eggs generally 10–12, sometimes 6 or 18; glossy surface, unmarked, ground colour olive-brown to olive-grey. Size 45·9 × 36·0 mm. Weight around 30 g. Incubation occasionally 23 days, usually 24–25. Single brood, March / April – June / July. Replacement clutch.
Nestlings yellowish-buff and rufous down; two long stripes (dark brown) running from the head down the back. Leave nest shortly after hatching.

CRANES   *Gruidae*

Associated with extensive areas of marsh and mere, with reedbeds and swamps of alder and willow. Nests are also found in damp meadows. Made out of old reeds, sedge or similar plants, the nest is often in the centre of a large area of flattened vegetation surrounded by knee-deep water; nesting material includes tussocks of grass, moss and stems of plants, but not branches. There is one brood per year, normally two eggs in a clutch. They are olive-green, with brown and dull grey blotches. One species breeds in central Europe; none in Br. Is. since the seventeenth century.

Crane *Grus grus*
(Not illustrated)
Site extensive reedbeds and alder or willow swamps, extending also into damp meadows. Nests are usually surrounded by knee-deep water.
Nest a large, flattened heap of old stems of reed and sedge, lined with additional bits of sedge, tussocks of grass and moss. (No branches.)
Eggs 2, rarely 3; olive-green

colour, marked with brown and grey blotches. Size 96·9 × 61·1 mm. Weight around 200 g. Incubation 29–31 days. Single brood, April–early May. Replacement clutch.
Nestlings down on upperparts rufous with paler patches, underparts whitish. Immediately after hatching they are able to swim, but not run, according to Heinroth. Remain in or near the nest for 9–10 weeks.

BUSTARDS   *Otididae*

Nests are on the ground in open steppe country in northern parts of range and among crops in large cultivated fields in the south. Little nesting material is used. The eggs are laid on the bare ground or in a scrape which is scantily lined with straw or grass. There is usually one brood per year with 2, sometimes 3, eggs, olive-green with brownish flecks and blotches. Two species breed in central Europe; none now breeds in Br. Is. but attempts are being made to reintroduce Great Bustard on Salisbury Plain.

Great Bustard *Otis tarda*
Pl. **53**

Site open grass steppes and large cultivated fields, among crops of cereals, roots, clover and rape.

Nest a bare scrape or one scantily lined with bits of local straw or grass.

Eggs 2, less often 3; olive-green or greyish-green ground colour, marked with brownish or ashen-grey blotches and flecks. Size 78·9 × 56·1 mm. Weight around 135 g. Incubation sometimes 23, usually 24–28 days. Single brood, late April–May; later records may represent replacement clutches.

Nestlings short thick down, brownish-yellow with pale patches and dark streaks. Leave nest shortly after hatching.

Little Bustard *Otis tetrax*
(Not illustrated)

Site open grass steppes or among crops of wheat, barley, clover and rape.

Nest similar bare or scantily lined scrape, as for Great Bustard.

Eggs 2–3, occasionally 4; very glossy surface, olive-green ground colour faintly clouded with brownish marks but may appear to be uniform olive-brown. Size 51·9 × 38·5 g. Weight 41 g. Incubation around 3 weeks. Single brood, May–June.

Nestlings slightly paler than Great Bustard. Leave nest shortly after hatching.

RAILS, CRAKES AND COOTS   *Rallidae*

Nests are usually in waterlogged sites, lodged in tussocks at water-level or not far above it, in tall growth of reeds or similar plants fringing sheets of water. Tall stems are often bent over to form a tent-like roofing. Nesting material consists of stems and leaves of local plants.

Key to the eggs: pale greyish-brown with blackish flecks (Coot); yellowish-white with lots of reddish-brown flecks (Corncrake); creamy-white with comparatively few reddish-brown and grey flecks (Water Rail); russet yellow to olive-brown with grey flecks, overlaid with brown blotches (Spotted Crake); greyish-buff dotted with reddish-brown flecks (Moorhen); yellowish-brown with reddish-brown blotches (Little Crake and Baillon's Crake). There are usually 6–8 eggs, sometimes 10, in a clutch and one to two broods per year. Seven species breed in central Europe; five of these breed regularly in Br. Is. (Little Crake and Baillon's Crake have not been recorded as breeding in recent years but nests are difficult to find and they are suspected breeders.)

Corncrake* *Crex crex*
Pl. **220**

Site favours comparatively dry ground with long grass. Often in hayfields, clover and other crops; also on waste ground where vegetation is tall enough to hide the nest.

Nest shallow depression lined with bits of dry grass and leaves.

Eggs usually 8–11, sometimes 6 or 12, occasionally 14; ground colour variable: yellowish-white, greyish-green, light reddish-brown. There are numerous reddish-brown and grey markings, similar to Water Rail except that they are more concentrated at the blunt end. Size 39·7 × 26·8 mm. Weight 13, occasionally 14–15 g. Incubation 14 to 18 days. Single brood, May/June –July. Replacement clutch.

Nestlings thick, blackish-bronze down; black bill, long and dark coloured toes. Leave nest shortly after hatching.

Moorhen* *Gallinula chloropus*
Pl. **29**

Site marshy ground near ponds or slow-flowing water, hidden in thick cover. Many nests are in tussocks of sedge or reeds, under tree-stumps or some other ground cover along the bank, others are in low branches, often over-hanging the water. Disused nests

of other species (such as Black-bird) are sometimes used.

Nest compactly built, stems of local plants are interlaced and lined with finer bits; tall sedge is sometimes bent over to hide the nest from above.

Eggs 6–10, rarely 11; greyish-buff ground colour dotted with dark reddish-brown flecks. Size 43·3 × 30·7 mm. Weight around 23 g. Incubation 20–21 days. Two broods, occasionally three, but eggs may be found in almost any month, peak season April–May.

Nestlings black down, bare red and blue patches are seen where down is sparse, particularly around the eyes; red bill has pale yellow tip, the red continues up the forehead as a 'shield'; legs and feet are black. Leave nest after a day or two, able to swim at once, able to fly after about 6 weeks.

Coot* *Fulica atra*
Pl. **30**

Site similar to Moorhen but Coot tends to nest near larger expanses of water with less cover along the banks. Some nests are surrounded by water, others have a tunnel-like runway leading up the bank.

Nest built on foundation of old or new growth of reeds, sedge and similar plants. The heap of local vegetation often forms a substantial structure of green bits mixed with dead bits.

Eggs 6–9, sometimes 4 or 10; pale greyish-brown ground colour dotted all over with chestnut and black flecks. Size 52·1 × 36·1 mm. Weight around 37·5 g. Incubation 21–23, rarely 24 days. Usually single-brooded, but up to three broods per year have been recorded, peak season April–June. Replacement clutch. *Nestlings* black down, orange-tipped on head and throat; red bill is white towards the tip, the red continuing up to the eyes. Able to leave nest after a day or two, do not become fully independent for about 8 weeks.

Water Rail* *Rallus aquaticus*
Pl. **27, 221**

Site waterlogged vegetation along margins of ditches, ponds, lakes and slow-flowing rivers; in dense cover of sedge, rush and reed, also in tall grass. Stems are often bent to form a tent-like roof, hiding the nest effectively from above. Nests may be just above water-level or lodged higher up in tussocks of tall vegetation.

Nest similar construction to Moorhen but a smaller version.

Eggs 6–11, less commonly 5 or 12; glossy surface, creamy-white ground colour with comparatively few reddish-brown and grey flecks. Size 36·1 × 26·2 mm. Weight 14 g. Incubation 19–20, sometimes 21 days. One or two broods per year, April–July. Replacement clutch.

Nestlings black down with bronze sheen; red patch on back of head; white bill is blackish at the tip. Able to leave nest shortly after hatching.

Spotted Crake* *Porzana porzana*
Pl. **212**

Site waterlogged or swampy ground with thick cover of reed-beds, sedge and rush; often along ditches, dykes and margins of ponds. Stems often form tent-like roof above the nest, as in Water Rail.

Nest loosely constructed out of a mixture of green and dead stems of local plants; inner depression about 5 cm deep.

Eggs 7 and 14 eggs recorded though 8–10 is usual; russet-yellow to olive-brown ground colour, marked with grey flecks overlaid by brown blotches. Size 33·6 × 24·0 mm. Weight about 10 g. Incubation 18–21 days. Two broods per year, early May–late July. Replacement clutch.

Nestlings black down with green sheen; flesh-coloured bill with red patch at base of upper mandible. Leave nest shortly after hatching.

Little Crake *Porzana parva*
Pl. **28, 213**

Site similar to Spotted Crake but favours tall reeds or high grass fringing expanses of water. Nests are well-hidden, mostly 10–50 cm above water-level but also up to 80 or 100 cm, and tall stems are often bent over to form tent-like roof. (Suspected breeding in Br. Is.)

Nest dry bits of sedge and rush, lined with dry grass.

Eggs sometimes 5, generally 6–8; yellowish-brown ground colour, overlaid with reddish-brown blotches. (The nest, illustrated in Pl. 28 was photographed in poor light, making the eggs appear too dark.) Size 30·7 × 22·0 mm. Weight around 8 g. Incubation 20–21 days. One or two broods per year, late May–July.

Nestlings black down with green sheen. Whitish bill and dark feet. Leave nest shortly after hatching.

Baillon's Crake *Porzana pusilla*
Pl. **210**

Site similar to other crakes but favours small pools with dense growth of sedge and reed. Nests are well-hidden and tall stems are often bent over, forming tent-like roof. (No breeding records in Br. Is. since mid-nineteenth century.)

Nest comparatively neat construction; rootlets, stems and leaves of sedge, etc. lined with finer, dry bits.

Eggs 6–8 most usual, sometimes 5; yellowish-brown ground colour, overlaid with reddish-brown blotches; very similar to Spotted Crake but smaller and darker. Size 28·9 × 20·6 mm. Weight 6·7 g. Incubation around 20 days. Two broods, May–July.

Nestlings leave nest shortly after hatching.

OYSTERCATCHERS *Haematopodidae*

Oystercatchers nest in scattered colonies, mainly along the seashore but also inland. Coastal sites include rock, shingle and sand; inland sites include cultivated fields and moorland some distance from water, as well as shingle banks of rivers and shores of lakes. The eggs are laid in a shallow scrape, which is often decorated with pebbles and shells. There are usually 3 eggs in a clutch, buff-grey to light brown with dark brown and grey markings, and one brood per year. One species breeds in central Europe and Br. Is.

Oystercatcher* *Haematopus ostralegus*
Pl. **37**

Site usually on seashore, less frequently inland and not necessarily close to water. Majority of nests are near the sea, on sand, rock or shingle. In some areas colonies are found on open moorland or in fields (short pasture or arable).

Nest shallow scrape which may be completely bare or scantily lined with bits of debris. Scrapes decorated with mussel shells are mostly 18–20 cm wide.

Eggs 2–4; buff-grey to light brown ground colour, marked with dark brown and grey streaks and blotches. Size 56·3 × 39·9 mm. Weight around 50 g. Incubation 26–28 days. Single brood, April/May–June/July.

Nestlings greyish-buff down on upperparts, white underparts. Leave nest after 1–2 days.

PLOVERS
Charadriidae

A number of waders belong to this family. Ringed Plover and Kentish Plover are typical seashore nesters, on sand or shingle; Little Ringed Plover favours freshwater, nesting on stony or waste ground, often near gravelpits; Dotterel and Golden Plover are typical of remote uplands, nesting on moorland; Lapwing, on the other hand, is typical of lowland areas, nesting on farmland and marshy ground. All these species make a simple scrape, relying more on protective coloration than on hiding the nest in ground cover. The eggs are pyriform and lie with the tapered end pointing to the centre; they are olive-brown, creamy-buff to greenish-yellow or yellowish-brown, with blackish markings. There are usually 3–4 eggs in a clutch and one to two broods per year. There are six breeding species in central Europe, all of which are recorded as nesting in Br. Is. (Kentish Plover now breeds only in the Channel Islands but may return to breed in southern England.)

Ringed Plover* *Charadrius hiaticula*
Pl. **31**

Site along the seashore on sand and shingle beaches or in dunes near the coast; less frequently inland on mud or stony ground by freshwater. Nests are usually out in the open, sometimes in sparse vegetation or near flotsam.
Nest shallow scrape, scantily decorated with small stones or shells, and sometimes a few bits of plant material.
Eggs 3–5, pyriform; greenish-grey or buff ground colour with grey streaks overlaid with dark brown spots. Markings tend to be concentrated at the tapered end. Size 35·7 × 25·9 mm. Weight 10 g. Incubation 23, although most commonly 24–27 days. One or two broods per year, April/May–July. Replacement clutch.
Nestlings short down, greyish-buff with various dark marks on upperparts, whitish underparts. Leave nest shortly after hatching.

Little Ringed Plover*
Charadrius dubius
Pl. **32, 211**

Site near freshwater on banks of gravel or shingle, dry mud or waste ground with little vegetation. Margins of gravelpits appear to attract this species. Nests are usually out in the open or half-hidden under sparse vegetation.
Nest small, shallow scrape, bare or decorated with small stones, bits of plants or debris.
Eggs 4, similar to Ringed Plover except for smaller size. Size 29·8 × 22·1 mm. Weight 6–8 g. Incubation 23–26 days. Two broods per year, April–July. Replacement clutch.
Nestlings short down, yellowish rather than greyish-buff, compared with Ringed Plover; also, a narrow black line across forehead. Leave nest shortly after hatching.

Kentish Plover* *Charadrius alexandrinus*
Pl. **33**
Site sand and shingle beaches by the sea, mussel-banks and flat dunes, saltings with short turf and expanses of mud; less frequently inland near freshwater or similar waste ground. (Breeds in Channel Islands.)
Nest shallow scrape, with or without decorative material. In some nests the eggs are half-buried by decorative or lining material.
Eggs 3; matt surface, stone or buff ground colour irregularly streaked and flecked with black markings. Size 33·1 × 23·5 mm. Weight around 9 g. Incubation 24–27 days. Single brood, May–June. Replacement clutch.
Nestlings short down which looks paler on upperparts than Ringed Plover owing to finer dark marks; white throat-band. Leave nest shortly after hatching.

Dotterel* *Eudromias morinellus*
Pl. **35**
Site exposed moors and hillsides with scree, rocky outcrops and stunted heather. (Mainly confined to Scottish Highlands.)
Nest shallow scrape, with or without lining of a few bits of grass, moss or lichen.
Eggs 2–4; olive-brown ground colour, heavily marked with blackish-brown blotches. Size 41·1 × 28·9 mm. Incubation 25, sometimes 27–28, days. Single brood, late May–July. Replacement clutch.
Nestlings thick down, cinnamon with black and white marbled

effect. Leave nest shortly after hatching.

Golden Plover* *Pluvialis apricaria*
Pl. **34**
Site peat moors on high ground, with bogs, shallow pools and typical vegetation of stunted heather, short grass and bog-cotton. (Also on northern tundra and Scandinavian fells.)
Nest shallow scrape in peat, with or without a few bits of heather, grass, etc.
Eggs 4; ground colour varies from creamy-buff to greenish-yellow or reddish-brown, marked with large brownish-black blotches. Size 51·8 × 35·9 mm. Weight around 34 g. Incubation 27 days. Single brood, April–May, or later in northern latitudes. Replacement clutch.
Nestlings long down, dark brown mottled with yellow, some white on the head. Leave nest shortly after hatching.

Lapwing* *Vanellus vanellus*
Pl. **38**
Site arable fields, damp pastures, marshes and moors. Nests are usually in the open or where ground cover is low.
Nest a depression, often on slightly raised site, lined with a few bits of grass stems or small bits of local plants.
Eggs 4, short pyriform; olive-brown ground colour with brownish-black flecks and blotches. Size 47·1 × 33·7 mm. Weight around 25 g. Incubation 24–26 days. Usually single-brooded,

late March–June, occasionally two broods. Replacement clutch. *Nestlings* mottled effect of black and brown down on upperparts, white throat-band. Leave nest shortly after hatching.

SANDPIPERS, GODWITS, CURLEWS AND SNIPE
Scolopacidae

The majority of nest-sites are in low ground cover in the vicinity of water. (Green Sandpiper is an exception and frequently uses tree-nests originally built by other species; Wood Sandpiper does so occasionally.) Nests are simple, little more than shallow depressions which are scantily lined with bits of grass and a few leaves. (Woodcock virtually covers the nest-hollow with dry leaves.) The majority of clutches have 4 eggs. The eggs lie with the tapered end pointing towards the centre of the nest. Ground colour varies according to species but all have dark markings.

Key to ground colour: bluish-green, yellowish or brownish-olive (Dunlin); greenish-grey (Temminck's Stint); yellowish-brown (Greenshank, Redshank, Common Sandpiper); greenish or greyish-green (Green Sandpiper, Wood Sandpiper, Turnstone). One brood per year, except for Woodcock which has two. Twelve species breed in central Europe. Eleven of these are also recorded as breeding in Br. Is.; some are very scarce and irregular, but there is no record of Turnstone having bred. In addition Whimbrel, which breeds regularly in Shetland, does not breed in central Europe.

Woodcock* *Scolopax rusticola*
Pl. **40**

Site woods or copses of underwood with open rides (for display-flight) and ground cover of bracken and bramble. Nests are on dry sites, often by the roots of a tree or in ground cover, but marshy ground (for feeding) is not far away.
Nest depression may be comparatively deep or a mere scrape; it is lined with dead leaves, sometimes also with grass.
Eggs 4, short ovate; light brown to warm brown ground colour marked with brown and purplish-grey flecks and blotches. Size 43·6 × 33·8 mm. Weight around 26 g. Incubation 20–22, sometimes 23 days. Two broods per year, March/April—June/July.
Nestlings marbled effect of rufous and yellowish-buff down. Leave nest shortly after hatching.

Snipe* *Gallinago gallinago*
Pl. **39**

Site marshes, moors, rough pastures and meadows. The actual nest-site may be dry but the surrounding vegetation is typical of marshy ground. Tussocks of grass, sedge, etc., effectively hide the nest from above.
Nest shallow depression, hidden by low vegetation, lined with bits of grass.

Eggs 3–5, pyriform; glossy surface; olive-brown ground colour marked with light and dark brown flecks and blotches. Size 39·3 × 28·6 mm. Weight 17–18 g. Incubation 19, occasionally 20–21 days. Single brood, April–June/July.

Nestlings tawny and black down, tipped white, giving a spangled appearance. Leave nest shortly after hatching.

Black-tailed Godwit* *Limosa limosa*
Pl. **42**

Site frequently in damp meadows and marshes, less often on moors, heaths and dunes. (Main site in Br. Is. is Ouse Washes in East Anglia.) Favours grassy hummocks near pools and marshy vegetation on margins of lakes.

Nest shallow depression lined with lots of dead grass and a few leaves, occasionally with debris.

Eggs 4; brownish-olive or greenish ground colour, marked with grey and dark brown streaks and spots. Size 54·7 × 37·5 mm. Weight around 40 g. Incubation 24 days. Single brood, April–May/June. Replacement clutch.

Nestlings pale brownish-grey down on upperparts (marbled pattern), greyish-white underparts. Leave nest shortly after hatching.

Curlew* *Numenius arquata*
Pl. **41**

Site favours lush meadows, damp pastures and marshy fields; also recorded in dry habitats (dunes and heaths). General terrain is usually damp but actual site is comparatively dry. Nests are well-hidden in low ground cover.

Nest shallow depression scantily lined with dry bits of local vegetation.

Eggs 3–5; brownish-olive or greenish ground colour, grey and dark brown markings tend to be concentrated at blunt end. Size 67·3 × 47·0 mm. Weight 65–85 g. Incubation around 28 days. Single brood, April–July. Replacement clutch.

Nestlings light and dark brown on upperparts (marbled pattern), paler brown underparts. Leave nest shortly after hatching.

Whimbrel* *Numenius phaeopus*
(Not illustrated)

Site boggy moorland with rough grass and stunted heather (Shetland); also in meadows, grassy verges of woodland, heathland and beyond tree-limit on open ground (N. Scandinavia).

Nest shallow depression, scantily lined with dry bits of local vegetation, hidden among hummocks and tussocks.

Eggs 4; similar to Curlew except for smaller size. Size 58·4 × 41·6 mm. Incubation about 24 days. Single brood, May–June. Replacement clutch.

Nestlings similar to Curlew except for two, clearly defined, dark stripes on crown. Leave nest shortly after hatching.

Ruff* *Philomachus pugnax*
Pl. **45**

Site damp meadows and marshy ground near brackish pools and freshwater in southern part of breeding range; on tundra in northern latitudes. Small numbers breed on Ouse Washes in East Anglia, larger populations on polders in Netherlands.

Nest shallow depression, lined with bits of grass, hidden among hummocks and tussocks.

Eggs sometimes 3, generally 4; ground colour varies from stone-grey to olive-brown, marked with pale grey and dark brown flecks and spots. Size 44·9 × 31·3 mm. Weight around 20 g. Incubation 21 days. Single brood, May–June.

Nestlings marbled effect of pinkish-buff, yellowish-buff and yellowish-white down; legs pinkish-grey. Leave nest shortly after hatching.

Dunlin* *Calidris alpina*
Pl. **44**

Site damp meadows and marshes near the coast, inland on high peat moors, and on tundra in northern latitudes. Nests are nearly always near water, often hidden under a tuft of grass.

Nest very neat hollow lined with dry grass and moss, sometimes with dead leaves.

Eggs 3–5; ground colour varies from bluish-green to yellowish- or brownish-olive, marked with dark brown blotches and pale grey shell-marks. Size 34·7 × 24·7 mm. Weight around 11 g. Incubation 17, occasionally 16–22 (?) days. Single brood, May–June/July.

Nestlings reddish and yellowish down on upperparts (marbled buff and black), whitish on underparts. Leave nest shortly after hatching.

Temminck's Stint* *Calidris temminckii*
(Not illustrated)

Site favours tundra-type habitat; shores and islets with boulders, short turf or low vegetation. Main breeding area is in northern latitudes (Scandinavia and Siberia) but has nested in England and Scotland.

Nest small, shallow depression scantily lined with dry grass and leaves.

Eggs 4, more rarely 5; greenish-grey ground colour with small dark flecks or larger stains. Size 28·0 × 20·4 mm. Weight around 6 g. Incubation 13–14 days. Single brood, June–July.

Nestlings buff and black down on upperparts (spangled pattern), whitish underparts. Leave nest shortly after hatching.

Common Sandpiper* *Tringa hypoleucos*
Pl. **230**

Site frequently associated with shores of lakes, lochs and hill streams where water has receded, occasionally some distance from water in comparatively open ground. Nest is usually hidden between plants that spring up on alluvial deposits; stones, pebbles and debris provide camouflage in the absence of plants.

Nest relatively deep depression scantily lined with bits of grass or local plants.

Eggs 4, pyriform; glossy surface;

ground colour varies from yellowish-brown to greyish-white, marked with dark flecks and spots. Size 36·3 × 26·0 mm. Weight 11–13 g. Incubation 21–22 days. Single brood, May–June. Replacement clutch.

Nestlings mottled effect of buff, grey and blackish down on upperparts, with one dark stripe along the back, white underparts; greenish-blue or pale grey-blue legs. Leave nest shortly after hatching.

Wood Sandpiper* *Tringa glareola*
Pl. **218**

Site damp meadows and boggy moors, usually on the ground in a dry patch, occasionally in tree-nests built by other species. (A few breed in Scotland.)

Nest a depression about 4 cm deep, scantily lined with bits of grass and leaves.

Eggs 4, pyriform; slightly glossy surface; pale green to olive-brown ground colour, dark markings (brown and red) tend to be concentrated at the blunt end. Size 38·3 × 27·0 mm. Weight around 13 g. Incubation 21–24 days. Single brood, May–June.

Nestlings greyish-white down with three dark stripes along the back; dark grey legs. Leave nest shortly after hatching.

Green Sandpiper* *Tringa ochropus*
Pl. **219**

Site trees on marshy ground near streams and lakes. Old nests

built by other species (Blackbird, Mistle Thrush, Song Thrush, Jay, Carrion Crow, Pigeon) are frequently taken over. (Sporadic in Br. Is., most likely area is Inverness.)

Nest usually a hollow scraped in old nest of other species; leaves or conifer needles may serve as lining material in an old nest or as the actual foundation of a new nest made by Green Sandpiper itself.

Eggs 4, pyriform; slightly glossy surface; ground colour varies from greenish-grey to buff or reddish-yellow; purplish-brown and grey markings tend to be concentrated at the blunt end. Size 39·1 × 28·0 mm. Weight around 16 g. Incubation 20–22 days. Single brood, late April–June. Replacement clutch.

Nestlings mottled effect of cinnamon and black down on upperparts, whitish-grey underparts. Remain in nest for 2 days, according to Heinroth, and then leap down to the ground.

Greenshank* *Tringa nebularia*
Pl. **235**

Site peat moors with heather, rock outcrops and runnels (Scottish Highlands), marshy glades in forests and open tundra (northern Scandinavia). Nests are usually well-hidden among low ground cover.

Nest a depression scantily lined with bits of vegetation or debris.

Eggs 4; yellowish-brown ground colour with reddish-brown spots and blotches. Size 51·4 × 34·8 mm. Weight 30·5 g. Incubation

24–25 days. Single brood, May–June.

Nestlings marbled effect of brown, grey and white down. Leave nest shortly after hatching.

Redshank* *Tringa totanus*
Pl. **43**

Site water meadows, rough pastures, marshes and moorland. Nests are often hidden under grass tussocks, with tall stems bent over to hide the nest from above.

Nest shallow depression scantily lined with a few bits of grass.

Eggs, 3–5, pyriform; yellowish-brown or buff ground colour, pale grey markings overlaid with dark brown spots and blotches. Size 44·3 × 31·2 mm. Weight around 22 g. Incubation 23–24 days. Single brood, April–June. Replacement clutch.

Nestlings yellowish-brown down on upperparts has a pattern of dark markings; white down on underparts has patches which are suffused with warm buff. Leave nest shortly after hatching.

Turnstone *Arenaria interpres*
Pl. **222**

Site usually associated with salt water, frequently on estuaries, coastal beaches and offshore islands with stony ground and poor vegetation; tundra and stony fells in far north. Nests are between stones or in patches of stranded flotsam on the coast.

Nest a depression lined with local plants; lining may be scanty or comparatively substantial.

Eggs sometimes 3, mostly 4, slightly pyriform; pale grey-green ground colour with ashen shell-marks overlaid with brown flecks and blotches. Size 39·7 × 28·9 mm. Weight 17·5 g. Incubation 23–27 days. Single brood, mid-May–June.

Nestlings marbled effect of yellowish-grey and black down on upperparts, dark patches on sides of throat, white underparts. Leave nest shortly after hatching.

AVOCETS AND STILTS *Recurvirostridae*

Avocets nest in loose colonies on saltmarshes, mudflats and low-lying meadows where there are shallow pools of saline or brackish water. Small groups of nests are found on slightly raised ground near water. The shallow depression is usually scantily lined with bits of local vegetation but may look bulky when reeds are used. The eggs are clay-buff, with grey and black markings; there are usually 4 in a clutch and one brood per year. There is only one species which breeds regularly in central Europe. A small population of Avocets breeds in East Anglia at the R.S.P.B.'s reserves at Havergate and Minsmere; larger populations breed in the Netherlands, particularly on the polders where reclaimed land provides suitable sites. (Black-winged Stilt *Himantopus himantopus* breeds sporadically in central Europe and in England.)

Avocet* *Recurvirostra avosetta*
Pl. **36**

Site usually near the coast on saltmarshes, sandbanks and mud-flats of estuaries or lagoons of brackish water; also in damp fields on reclaimed land. Small groups nest on tussocks of vegetation.

Nest shallow depression lined with bits of local vegetation; amount of lining material varies.

Eggs 2–5; clay-buff ground colour with ash-grey shell-marks and blackish-brown flecks which are concentrated at the blunt end. Size 50·6 × 35·1 mm. Weight 30–32 g. Incubation 23–24 days. Single brood, late April–June. Replacement clutch.

Nestlings sandy coloured down with dark marbled patterns on upperparts, pale grey under-parts; characteristic curve of bill is recognisable in chick. Leave nest shortly after hatching.

PHALAROPES   *Phalaropodidae*

Phalaropes are usually sociable breeders. They nest on the coast on damp, grassy ground or on moorland near shallow pools. Eggs are laid in a small hollow, scraped in a tussock and scantily lined with a few bits of dead grass. There are usually 4 eggs in a clutch and one brood per year. The eggs are stone-grey to olive-green, marked with brown flecks. One species breeds in parts of northern Europe, including north Scotland and north-west Ireland.

Red-necked Phalarope*
Phalaropus lobatus
Pl. **209**

Site grassy places near the coast and wet moorland near shallow pools or lochs. There is often more than one nest in the area.

Nest shallow depression, often on raised hummock, lined with dry grass.

Eggs most commonly 4, some-times 3; stone-grey to olive-green ground colour with dark brown flecks. Size 29·9 × 21·0 mm. Weight 6·3 g. Incubation 20–21 days. Single brood, May–July.

Nestlings various shades of buff, brown and black down. Leave nest shortly after hatching.

THICKNEES   *Burhinidae*

Stone Curlew is associated with stony or sandy soil where there is very little ground cover. The nest is usually in the open, between rather than under any plant growth, and the shallow depression is virtually unlined; there may be a few bits of debris, rabbit droppings or small pebbles as decoration. There are 2 eggs in a clutch and one brood per year. The eggs are stone-grey or sandy colour, strongly marked with irregular blackish-brown streaks and blotches. Only one member of this family breeds in central Europe, including a few counties in England.

Stone Curlew* *Burhinus oedicnemus*
(Not illustrated)

Site dunes, heaths, downs, arable and waste ground, on stony or sandy soil. Recorded among young conifers but usually on open ground with little or no cover.
(Now confined to East Anglia and a few counties in southern England.)

Nest shallow scrape, unlined, sometimes decorated with small stones or animal droppings (hare or rabbit).

Eggs 2; stone-grey or sandy ground colour, irregularly streaked and blotched with blackish-brown markings. Size 53·8 × 38·4 mm. Weight around 37 g. Incubation sometimes 23, generally 25–27 days. Single brood, April / May – July / August. Replacement clutch.

Nestlings sandy-buff down, with narrow dark stripes on upperparts; greyish underparts. Leave nest shortly after hatching.

PRATINCOLES
Glareolidae

Nesting colonies are found on waste ground in short grass or steppe-type vegetation, often in vicinity of water. The nest is a shallow depression without any lining material. There are usually 3 eggs in a clutch and one brood per year. The eggs are sandy brown, heavily marked with dark flecks and blotches. There is one breeding species in southern Europe which does not breed in Br. Is.

Pratincole *Glareola pratincola*
Pl. 1

Site waste ground, short grass or steppe-type vegetation. Colonies are in places 'baked' by the sun in the vicinity of water.

Nest shallow scrape, no lining or decorative material. (Illustration shows eggs lying in hoofmark of cattle.)

Eggs 3, less commonly 2; sandy ground colour with marbled pattern of dark brown or black markings. Size 32·9 × 24·1 mm. Weight around 10 g. Incubation about 17–18 days. Single brood, May–June.

Nestlings sandy-buff and dark brown down on upperparts, pinkish and buff on underparts. Leave nest shortly after hatching.

SKUAS
Stercorariidae

Scattered colonies and some single nests are found on moorland and tundra, usually near the sea, sometimes near inland water. The nest is a shallow depression with little or no lining material. There are usually 2 eggs and one brood per year. The eggs are brown to olive-green with large, dark blotches. Two species breed in northern parts of Europe, including N. Scotland.

Arctic Skua* *Stercorarius parasiticus*
Pl. **250**

Site northern moorland, usually near the sea but also inland near lochs, on offshore islands (Orkney and Shetland), and on tundra in far north. Nests are mostly in small groups or scattered colonies.

Nest shallow depression with little or no lining material, sometimes a bit of dry grass or moss.

Eggs 2, occasionally 3; olive-green to olive-brown ground colour with dark brown or purplish markings. Size 57·2 × 40·2 mm. Weight 50 g. Incubation 25–26 days. Single brood, late May–July.

Nestlings blackish-brown down on upperparts, paler underparts.

Able to leave nest shortly after hatching.

Great Skua* *Stercorarius skua*
(Not illustrated)

Site similar to Arctic Skua, usually in scattered colonies but isolated nests are also found.

Nest shallow depression with little or no lining material, sometimes a bit of dry grass or moss.

Eggs 2; greyish to olive-brown ground colour, with dark brown or black markings. Size 70·6 × 49·2 mm. Incubation 29–30 days. Single brood, mid-May–early July.

Nestlings yellowish-brown down on upperparts, paler underparts. Able to leave nest shortly after hatching.

GULLS   *Laridae*

The majority of Gulls nest along the coast in colonies, large or small, and the nesting terrain may be steep or flat. Sites include cliffs, sand or shingle beaches, dunes, marshes and moors. Nests are usually on the ground but trees and ledges of buildings are also recorded. Inland sites are near lakes or pools. Nesting material includes any local material available: grass, straw, moss, seaweed or sticks flattened into a shallow depression in the centre, though the nest may be quite bulky. The eggs are marked with grey or dark brown spots and flecks; ground colour varies from olive-green to deep brown, and from buff to yellowish, bluish, or stone grey. The majority of clutches have 3 eggs and there is one brood per year. Six species breed in central Europe and in Br. Is.

Kittiwake* *Rissa tridactyla*
(Not illustrated)

Site typically on inaccessible cliffs overlooking the sea but also recorded on low cliffs, flat ground and ledges of buildings. Colonies on steep cliffs are usually large.

Nest compared with other Gulls, the nest-bowl is much deeper. Nesting material includes grass, seaweed and moss.

Eggs 1–3; ground colour varies from bluish-grey, yellowish-grey, stone grey to brownish, with pale grey and brown markings. Size 54·8 × 40·2 mm. Weight around 45 g. Incubation 21–26 days. Single brood, late May–July. Replacement clutch.

Nestlings comparatively long down, greyish-brown on upperparts, white underparts, creamy white on head and throat. Remain in nest for about 4 weeks.

Black-headed Gull* *Larus ridibundus*
Pl. **2**

Site usually on waterlogged or very damp ground near pools or lochs, in tussocks of rush and sedge or on hummocks of short grass. Sites include marshes, moors, dunes and shingle banks. Colonies vary in size and some are quite far inland.

Nest made out of any available bits of vegetation.

Eggs 3, sometimes 2, ground colour varies from pale blue or olive-green to deep brown, marked with greyish-purple flecks overlaid by dark brown blotches. Size 52·3 × 36·9 mm. Weight around 38 g. Incubation 23 days. Single brood, late April–June/July. Replacement clutch.

Nestlings marbled pattern of reddish-brown and blackish-brown down on upperparts, pale underparts; characteristic flesh-coloured bill with dark tip and two black patches on the throat. Leave nest after a few days and run around in the colony.

Common Gull* *Larus canus*
Pl. **5**

Site among low vegetation on shingle and dunes in sheltered parts of the coast and inland on moorland near freshwater lochs. Some colonies are extensive but this species appears to be more selective than other Gulls and avoids exposed parts of the coast. Nests are usually on the ground, but there are records that nests originally built by other species in trees have been used. Breeding colonies in Br. Is. are mainly confined to Scotland and Ireland.

Nest size varies from a bulky construction of heather, sedge, reeds, grass, moss and feathers to a shallow depression, sparsely lined.

Eggs 2–4; ground colour varies from pale blue or green to olive-brown, marked with dark grey and black streaks and flecks. Size 58·6 × 41·8 mm. Weight 56 g. Incubation 21–24 days. Single brood, late April/May–June/July. Replacement clutch.

Nestlings marbled pattern of pale grey and black down on upperparts; contrast of pale and dark down is more marked than in previous species and there are no distinctive throat-patches. Leave nest after a few days but remain in colony.

Herring Gull* *Larus argentatus*
Pl. **4**

Site usually on cliffs overlooking the sea, less frequently on shingle and dunes, and occasionally inland near freshwater; also recorded locally on seaside buildings and in trees. Colonies vary in size; individual nests may be well spaced out.

Nest size varies from a mere

scrape, scantily lined and easily overlooked, to a comparatively bulky structure made out of local vegetation, such as grass, seaweed, lichen or moss.

Eggs sometimes 2, generally 3; ground colour varies from olive-green to stone-grey or brown, marked with blackish flecks, streaks and hook-marks. Size 70·9 × 49·0 mm. Weight 92 g. Incubation 26–28 days. Single brood, late April/May–June/July. Replacement clutch.

Nestlings marbled pattern of pale greyish-buff and black down on upperparts; two black patches on throat. Leave nest after a few days but remain in colony.

Lesser Black-backed Gull*
Larus fuscus
Pl. **3**

Site grassy slopes and steep cliffs overlooking the sea, low islets with short turf. There are also inland colonies on boggy moorland. Local records of nests built in bushes, trees and on buildings.

Nest amount of material varies; made out of bits of local vegetation, grass, seaweed, heather, etc.

Eggs 2–4; ground colour varies from greenish-grey to dark brown, marked with dark grey and blackish flecks, scrawls and hook-marks. Size 66·8 × 46·2 mm. Weight 87 g, 80–100 g also recorded. Incubation 23–27 days. Single brood, May–June/July. Replacement clutch.

Nestlings very similar to Herring Gull and difficult to tell apart when running about.

Great Black-backed Gull*
Larus marinus
Pl. **6**

Site usually on steep cliffs overlooking the sea, less frequently inland on boggy moorland. Isolated nests occur as well as colonies.

Nest comparatively bulky, made out of dry grass, seaweed, sticks or any available local material; sometimes a few feathers are also part of the lining.

Eggs 2–4; ground colour varies from stone-grey or buff to olive-brown, marked with brown flecks, streaks and scrawls. Size 76·6 × 53·9 mm. Weight 116 g. Incubation 26–28 days. Single brood, April/May–June. Replacement clutch.

Nestlings marbled pattern of pale grey and brown down, conspicuous brown and black markings on head, back and throat. Able to leave nest after a few days but remain in the vicinity.

TERNS
Sternidae

Tern colonies are found along the seashore on sand and shingle beaches and inland near freshwater. Except for Black Tern which often builds a 'floating platform', nests are mere scrapes in the ground, often without any lining or decorative material. There are usually 2–3 eggs and one brood per year. The ground colour varies from creamy-white, buff or grey to greenish and shades of brown, with grey and dark brown flecks and shell-marks. There are six breeding species; Roseate Tern is absent from most of central Europe and Black Tern only nests sporadically in England.

Black Tern* *Chlidonias niger*
Pl. 7

Site in shallow water of fens and swamps or on boggy ground near freshwater pools. Small colonies or isolated pairs are often in the vicinity of breeding colonies of Black-headed Gulls and Black-necked Grebes. (Sporadic breeder in East Anglia.)

Nest flattened heap, either 'floating' or on firm hummock; bits of reed and sedge or aquatic weeds may be added but the depression for the eggs is· very shallow.

Eggs occasionally 2, generally 3; yellow-ochre, brownish or olive ground colour, marked with ash-grey flecks overlaid with brownish-black blotches. Size 34·6 × 25·0 mm. Weight around 11 g. Incubation 17 days. Single brood, mid-May–early June. Replacement clutch.

Nestlings mottled pattern of reddish and black down on upperparts, lilac-grey underparts. Remain in or near nest at first, able to fly after about 3 weeks.

Sandwich Tern* *Sterna sandvicensis*
Pl. 12

Site usually along the coast or on offshore islets, sand or shingle beaches and dunes; less frequently inland near freshwater. Large colonies nest among sparse vegetation.

Nest shallow depression, scantily lined with a few bents or bits of seaweed.

Eggs 1–3; ground colour varies from creamy-white to brown, strongly marked with purplish-grey and blackish-brown scrawls and spots. Size 51·7 × 36·1 mm. Weight 36–40 g. Incubation about 23 days. Single brood, early May–June/July. Replacement clutch.

Nestlings yellowish-grey down on upperparts with some darker mottling, whitish underparts. Remain in or near nest at first, able to fly after about 5 weeks.

Common Tern* *Sterna hirundo*
Pl. 8

Site coastal beaches, sand or shingle, and dunes; also on low, rocky islets and inland on gravel banks of rivers or shores of freshwater lochs where vegetation is sparse. Nests in colonies, sometimes in mixed colonies with next species.

Nest shallow depression, unlined or with a few bits of grass or seaweed.

Eggs 2–4, ground colour varies from creamy to olive-brown or greenish, marked with large grey flecks overlaid with plenty of dark brown blotches. Size 41·0 × 30·3 mm. Weight around 20 g. Incubation 23–24 days. Single brood May–June/July. Replacement clutch.

Nestlings yellowish-green down on upperparts with black mottling, white underparts. Remain in or near nest at first, able to fly at about 3 weeks.

Arctic Tern* *Sterna paradisaea* Pl. **9, 10**

Site similar to Common Tern; favours flat beaches and shores with sparse vegetation; also on low, rocky islands and inland near freshwater. Nests in colonies. *Nest* shallow depression, unlined or with a few bits of dry grass, etc. *Eggs* 1–3; ground colour varies from pale buff to grey or greyish-brown, grey shell-marks overlaid with blackish-brown blotches. Some eggs are heavily marked (see Pl. 9). Size 40·2 × 29·4 mm. Weight 19 g. Incubation 20–22 days. Single brood, late April/May—June/July. Replacement clutch.
Nestlings very similar to Common Tern but sometimes a dusky patch shows up across the forehead. Remain in or near nest at first, able to fly after about 3 weeks.

Roseate Tern* *Sterna dougallii* (Not illustrated)

Site sand and shingle beaches along the coast or on offshore islets. Apparently more selective than two previous species as colonies are not established inland. Pairs of Roseate Terns are sometimes found scattered among coastal colonies of Arctic and Common Terns.
Nest shallow depression, often in a natural hollow; lining material usually scanty but some nests are decorated with bits of bracken, flower-heads, moss or rabbit droppings.
Eggs 1–2, occasionally 3; ground colour varies from cream to pale brown, strongly marked with chestnut and ash-grey flecks. Size 44·0 × 30·0 mm. Incubation 21 days. Single brood, June–July. Replacement clutch.
Nestlings mottled pattern of yellowish-buff, warm buff and black down on upperparts, white underparts. Leave nest shortly after hatching but remain in vicinity of nest, able to fly after about 4 weeks.

Little Tern* *Sterna albifrons* Pl. **11**

Site sand and shingle beaches along the coast, mudflats with sparse vegetation, and sometimes near freshwater inland. Colonies are usually small.
Nest shallow depression, usually unlined but occasionally decorated with a few pebbles or shells.
Eggs 2–3, sometimes 4; pale sandy or brownish-yellow ground colour, marked with small dark flecks of purplish-grey and black. Size 32·9 × 23·8 mm. Weight around 10 g. Incubation 20–22 days. Single brood, May–June/July. Replacement clutch.
Nestlings mottled pattern of dark brown and yellow down on upperparts, greyish-white underparts. Leave nest shortly after hatching but remain in vicinity of nest, able to fly after about 4 weeks.

AUKS

Alcidae

Auks build no nest but lay their eggs on inaccessible rock ledges (Razorbill and Guillemot), in holes and crevices among boulders (Black Guillemot), or in burrows near the sea which they excavate themselves (Puffin). Only one egg is laid, except for Black Guillemot which lays two, and there is only one brood per year. The ground colour of the eggs may be white, buff or greenish-blue; markings are grey or very dark. (Variation in colour and marking is strongest in Guillemot.) Four species breed in northern Europe and in Br. Is.

Puffin* *Fratercula arctica*
Pl. **247**

Site grassy slopes of mainland cliffs and islands where the soil between rocks is suitable for excavating breeding burrows. Sometimes burrows originally occupied by rabbits or Manx Shearwaters are taken over. Colonies are usually large.

Nest virtually no nesting material is taken into the nesting chamber which is at the end of the burrow.

Egg 1; whitish ground colour, with faint brown and grey flecks; egg soon becomes stained. Size 60·9 × 42·3 mm. Weight 57–67 g. Incubation 40–42 days. Single brood, April/May–July.

Nestling a mixture of blackish, grey and brown down with white central panel on underparts. Remains in burrow for about 40 days and then makes own way to sea.

Razorbill* *Alca torda*
(Not illustrated)

Site steep cliffs with rock ledges and crevices overlooking the sea, also on lower part of cliff where there are boulders and slabs of rock. Suitable ledges may have colonies of Razorbills and Guillemots nesting side by side, but

Razorbills tend to be in sheltered crevices.

Nest no nesting material; egg is laid on bare rock, often in a hole or crevice where debris may accumulate.

Egg 1; ground colour varies from whitish to buff, heavily marked with dark blotches. Size 73·1 × 46·9 mm. Weight 70–98 (100) g. Incubation 25 days. Single brood, April/May–June/July.

Nestling a mixture of brownish-black and buff down with white central panel on underparts. Leaves cliff for first time when about 2 weeks old.

Guillemot* *Uria aalge*
Pl. **13, 248**

Site similar to Razorbill, but favours open ledges. Nesting colonies of Razorbills, Guillemots and Kittiwakes may all be found on one cliff overlooking the sea.

Nest no nesting material; egg is laid on bare rock, usually on open ledge rather than in a hole or crevice.

Egg 1, long pyriform; ground colour very variable, including whitish, greenish'or pale blue and buff, marked with dark blotches and scrawls. Size 81·5 × 49·7 mm. Weight 98–140 g. Incubation 28–30 days. Single brood, April/May–July.

Nestling a mixture of black, brown, grey and white down. Leaves cliff for first time when about 2 weeks old.

Black Guillemot* *Cepphus grylle*
Pl. **236**

Site on rocky coasts where there are crevices and clefts towards the base of the cliff or boulders and rocks on the shore. There may be small colonies or isolated pairs.

Nest no nesting material, eggs lie hidden in crevices where debris may accumulate.

Eggs 1–3, ovate; ground colour varies from bluish-green to buff-white, marked with various spots and blotches which are grey and black or reddish-brown. Size 58·1 × 39·5 mm. Weight 40–50 g. Incubation sometimes 21 (?) days, generally 27–28 days. Single brood, May–June/July.

Nestlings blackish-brown down on upperparts, paler shade on underparts. Go to sea after about 34 days.

PIGEONS AND DOVES   *Columbidae*

Nests are built in trees and bushes (Wood Pigeon, Collared Dove, Turtle Dove) or in a hole of some kind; holes may be in old trees, buildings or cliffs (Stock Dove, Rock Dove). Nests are flat and flimsy, loosely constructed out of twigs or sticks and without any special decoration or lining. There are usually 2 eggs in a clutch, glossy white, and there are two to three broods per year. Five species breed in central Europe and Br. Is.

Wood Pigeon* *Columba palumbus*
Pl. **61**

Site at varying heights in outer branches of trees (conifers and hardwoods) and in bushes or untrimmed hedgerows. Derelict nest of other species, mainly of the Crow family, or old squirrel drey, is sometimes used as a foundation.

Nest flimsy 'platform' of loosely arranged sticks or dry twigs, no special lining material.

Eggs 2, less often 3; glossy surface, pure white. Size 40·1 × 28·7 mm. Weight 18–19 g. Incubation 15½–17, rarely 18 days. Usually two to three broods per

year, March–July, sometimes a fourth in September, but clutches may be found in any month.

Nestlings bare patches of bluish-pink skin and yellowish down. Leave nest after 3–4 weeks.

Stock Dove* *Columba oenas*
(Not illustrated)

Site at varying heights in some kind of hole often at a height of 10–25 m up a tree, either in a natural hole or one originally excavated by a Woodpecker; also in nestboxes and in rabbit burrows. Several pairs may nest in the same vicinity.

Nest there may be little or no nesting material in the hole but sometimes there is a flat, loose arrangement of twigs, leaves, moss and fibrous roots.

Eggs 2, sometimes 3; glossy surface, pure white. Size 37·9 × 29·0 mm. Weight 16 g. Incubation 16–17 days. Two broods regularly, March–August, and often three or four.

Nestlings similar to Wood Pigeon but down is a richer colour. Leave nest after 18–24 days.

Rock Dove* *Columba livia*
(Not illustrated)

Site holes and fissures in rocky cliffs, usually overlooking the sea, sometimes in caves; several pairs nest in the same vicinity. Feral populations also nest inland on buildings.

Nest very little material in nest-hole; there may be just a few dead twigs, grass or straw.

Eggs 2; glossy surface, pure white. Size 39·3 × 29·1 mm. Weight around 17 g. Incubation 17 days. Two to three broods per year, March–July, and often a fourth. Protracted breeding season like other members of the family.

Nestlings yellowish down. Leave nest after 4–5 weeks.

Collared Dove* *Streptopelia decaocto*
(Not illustrated)

Site at varying heights in trees and bushes, mostly 8–16 m above the ground but also from 4–5 m. Also colonises artificial sites such as telegraph poles and buildings.

Nest typical Pigeon's nest but smaller than other species; a loose, flimsy platform of twigs or sticks, lined with grass and rootlets.

Eggs 2; glossy surface, pure white. Size 31·9 × 24·0 mm. Weight 8–9 g. Incubation sometimes 14, commonly 15–16 days. Two to three broods per year, early March–October, sometimes four and occasionally five.

Nestlings yellowish down. Leave nest after about 15 days.

Turtle Dove* *Streptopelia turtur*
(Not illustrated)

Site majority of nests are low down, 1–4 m above ground, in young plantations of conifers or hardwoods, untrimmed hedgerows and bramble thickets. Nests are in small copses rather than extensive stands of trees.

Nest flimsy platform of twigs, sometimes built on foundation of old nest of other species (e.g. Song Thrush).

Eggs 2, occasionally 3; glossy surface, pure white. Size 30·7 × 23·0 mm. Weight 9 g. Incubation 13–15 days. One to two broods per year May–June/July. Replacement clutch.

Nestlings bare patches of pink skin and yellowish down. Leave nest after about 15 days.

CUCKOOS
Cuculidae

There are about 130 members of this family, of which 50 have parasitic breeding habits. The Cuckoo which breeds in central Europe and Br. Is. builds no nest of its own, but lays eggs in the nests of other species. Many species fulfil the role of foster-parents, including Dunnock, Meadow Pipit, Pied Wagtail, Robin, Red-backed Shrike, Wren and various Warblers. The Cuckoo's eggs may be larger than the eggs of the foster-parent, but often resemble them. One female cuckoo lays about 12–16 eggs, although up to 22 have been recorded in a season, spread over a period of about 34–46 days.

Cuckoo* *Cuculus canorus*
Pl. **77, 85, 201, 202**

Site according to the species which is parasitised.

Nest no nest of its own; eggs are laid in various nests built by other species.

Eggs 12–16, exceptionally 22; colour and marking variable; often each egg resembles the eggs in the nest of the foster-parent (see Nest Parasitism, page 22). Size 22·4 × 16·5 mm. Weight around 3 g. Eggs are laid at intervals of 2–3 days, according to Heinroth. The laying period lasts for about 36–46 days and coincides with the breeding season of the foster-parents, May–early July. Incubation by foster-parents 12½ days.

Nestlings naked at first, pink skin turns blackish. According to Heinroth, ten hours after hatching the young cuckoo ejects any eggs or young from the fosterer's nest, and it remains in the nest for 22–23 days.

OWLS
Strigidae

Owls generally do not build a nest of their own but lay their eggs in natural holes, mostly in trees, or in nests built by other species. Short-eared Owl builds its own nest on the ground; Long-eared Owl also does so on occasion. The eggs of all species are white and short ovate, except for Barn Owl which are ovate. There is one brood per year. Clutch-size varies with the availability of prey; 4–6 eggs are laid in a normal year but in a 'lemming' year, or when other prey species are abundant, there are 6–8, and occasionally 10, per clutch. Ten species breed in central Europe, five of which also breed in Br. Is. (In addition, Snowy Owl *Nyctea scandiaca*, which breeds in Shetland, is not listed below.)

Eagle Owl *Bubo bubo*
(Not illustrated)

Site natural rock clefts and fissures, hollows in the ground among low cover, and in tall trees where old nests of other species are taken over (Heron, Buzzard, Osprey). Few natural holes in trees are sufficiently large for this species which is the largest owl in Europe.

Nest no nesting material. Moulted feathers and mammal remains (hair and bones) lie around, forming a circle around eggs laid on the ground.

Eggs 2–3, sometimes 4; short ovate, white. Size 59·8 × 49·5 mm. Weight around 80 g. Incubation 34–36 days. Single brood, early April.

Nestlings whitish down at first, becoming greyish-yellow after 5–6 weeks. Remain in nest for 5 weeks.

Scops Owl *Otus scops*
(Not illustrated)

Site natural holes in trees; favours trees in comparatively open situations, such as in avenues, at the edges of plantations or on the banks of rivers. Less frequently in old nests of other species (Crow, Magpie) and holes in old walls or rock-clefts.

Nest no nesting material.

Eggs 3–4, occasionally 5, short ovate; white. Size 31·3 × 27·0 mm. Weight around 12 g. Incubation 24–25 days. Single brood, May–mid June.

Nestlings creamy-buff down on upperparts with dark brown lines and patches; whiter on underparts. Remain in nest for about 4 weeks.

Long-eared Owl* *Asio otus*
Pl. **62**

Site old nests of other species, usually Carrion Crow, Magpie

and Pigeon, but occasionally Sparrowhawk, Heron and squirrels' dreys; seldom a natural hole in tree or on the ground.

Nest takes over old nests of other species.

Eggs 4–6, short ovate; white. Size 40·9 × 32·7 mm. Weight around 23 g. Incubation 27–28 days. Single brood, March–April, except in years of abundant prey when there may be a second brood, May–June.

Nestlings short white down, pink skin. Remain in nest for 21–24 days.

Short-eared Owl* *Asio flammeus*
Pl. **54**

Site marshes with reed, rush and sedge; open moorland with heather, sand-dunes with marram grass and sandy heathland. Nest is in open situation but well-hidden by ground cover.

Nest unlike other Owls this species builds its own nest. Nest consists of a depression in the ground, scantily decorated with bits of trampled grass or stems of local vegetation. The eggs, as shown in the illustration, are laid in a mere scrape.

Eggs 4–7 in normal year, 8–11 when prey is abundant; white. Size 40·1 × 31·8 mm. Weight 21–22 g. Incubation 26–27 days. Single brood, March/April–June/July.

Nestlings short greyish-yellow or buff-down, reddish skin. Remain in nest for 17 days.

Ural Owl *Strix uralensis*
(Not illustrated)
Site usually in hollow trees, often where branches have split from the trunk and left a large fissure; sometimes in old nests of Birds of Prey.
Nest no building material used.
Eggs 3–4, more rarely 5; white. Size 49·4 × 41·9 mm. Weight around 48 g. Incubation 27–29 days. Single brood, late February–May.
Nestlings remain in nest for 4–5 weeks.

Tawny Owl* *Strix aluco*
(Not illustrated)
Site frequently in hollow trees, less frequently in church towers or holes in old buildings, occasionally in nests of other species, Buzzard, Crow, Magpie, squirrels' dreys. Tunnel-type nest-boxes are used.
Nest no building material used. Eggs are laid on bare floor or debris in nest-hole.
Eggs 2–5, mostly 2 or 3, short ovate; white. Size 48·2 × 38·7 mm. Weight around 39 g. Incubation 28–29 days. Single brood, late February–May.
Nestlings white down. Remain in nest for 4–5 weeks.

Tengmalm's Owl *Aegolius funereus*
(Not illustrated)
Site old nest-holes of Black Woodpecker, particular in spruce or pine, also in other natural holes in trees and occasionally in nest-boxes. The nest-site is often very high.

Nest no nesting material.
Eggs 5–6, less commonly 4 or 7; white. Size 32·3 × 26·3 mm. Weight around 12·4 g. Incubation 26–28 days. Single brood, mid-March–early May.
Nestlings short white down. Remain in nest for 31–36 days.

Little Owl* *Athene noctua*
(Not illustrated)
Site holes in trees, particularly pollard willows, old poplars and decaying branches of old fruit-trees; also nests in holes in walls of old buildings, particularly on farmland. Occasionally uses nest-boxes.
Nest no nesting material.
Eggs 3–5, sometimes 6, short ovate; white without any gloss. Size 33·6 × 28·1 mm. Weight around 15–16 g. Incubation 28 days. Single brood, April–June.
Nestlings short white down. Remain in nest for 4 weeks.

Pygmy Owl *Glaucidium passerinum*
(Not illustrated)
Site natural holes in trees, particularly in conifer plantations, and often in nest-hole of Great Spotted Woodpecker.
Nest no nesting material.
Eggs 4–6; white, slightly glossy. Size 28·8 × 22·8 mm. Weight around 8·3 g. Incubation 28 days. Single brood, late April–May.
Nestlings remain in nest for 29–32 days.

Barn Owl* *Tyto alba*
(Not illustrated)
Site hollow trees, holes in derelict walls and church towers, also in

barns and lofts. Ledge-type nest-boxes are used.

Nest no nesting material; remnants of prey and other debris accumulate.

Eggs sometimes 3, usually 4–7; ovate; white without any gloss. Size 39·2 × 30·8 mm. Weight 20·7 g. Incubation 30, less commonly 34 days. Single brood, March–August, except in years of abundant prey when there may be a second brood.

Nestlings sparse white down, replaced by creamy down. Remain in nest for about 60 days.

NIGHTJARS   *Caprimulgidae*

European Nightjar does not build a nest. The eggs are laid on the bare ground. There are normally 2 eggs in a clutch: whitish with grey and brown marbled pattern. There are two broods per year. One species breeds regularly in central Europe and Br. Is.

Nightjar* *Caprimulgus europaeus*
Pl. **131**

Site among dead leaves or previous year's debris on woodland floor, in clearings or young plantations; also on rough ground of heaths, commons and dunes.

Nest no nesting material although there may be dead bracken, leaves and sticks lying around.

Eggs 2, elliptical; greyish-white with grey and brown marbled pattern. Size 31·9 × 22·5 mm. Weight 8 g. Incubation 17–18 days. Two broods, May–August.

Nestlings yellowish-brown which merges with surroundings. Remain in nest until they are able to fly, after about 3 weeks.

SWIFTS   *Apodidae*

Swifts are hole-nesters. They breed in small or large colonies. Two species breed in central Europe: Swift and Alpine Swift. In Br. Is. Swift favours holes in buildings but also nests in cliff crevices; in Europe holes in trees are also occupied. Alpine Swift, which does not breed in Br. Is., favours crevices in cliffs. Loose bits of nesting material such as straw, hair and feathers are 'glued' together with saliva. There are usually 2 eggs in a clutch, long elliptical, pure white, and one brood per year.

Swift* *Apus apus*
(Not illustrated)

Site favours holes in tall buildings, such as church towers and ruins, less frequently in crevices or niches of cliffs. Occasionally takes over old nests of other species and sometimes uses nestboxes. Holes in trees are also used regularly on the Continent. Swift colonies are usually on their own but from time to time the same site is shared with the next species.

Nest material collected in flight

is flattened and 'glued' together with saliva into a shallow 'saucer'; this consists of bits of animal hair, feathers, straw and fibrous material. Sometimes the nest is built on top of an old nest of other species, such as House Sparrow.

Eggs 2, less often 3, long elliptical; white without any gloss. Size 25·0 × 16·3 mm. Weight 3·6 g. Incubation 18–20 days. Single brood, May–June/July. Replacement clutch.

Nestlings no down, pinkish skin; flesh-colour inside mouth, white gape-flanges. Period in nest varies from 30–54, and sometimes 56 days.

Alpine Swift *Apus melba*
(Not illustrated)

Site unlike the previous species rock crevices and fissures are favoured, but colonies are also found in holes in walls, under eaves and rafters of tall buildings, including church towers.

Nest more solidly built but otherwise similar to previous species.

Eggs 1–3, long elliptical; white without any gloss. Size 31·1 × 19·3 mm. Weight around 6·7 g. Incubation 19–20 days. Single brood, late May–June.

Nestlings remain in nest about 42 days, although 30–54 days not unknown.

KINGFISHERS *Alcedinidae*

A tunnel-type nesting burrow is excavated in steep banks of rivers and streams. It is enlarged at the far end to form a nest-chamber. No nesting material is carried in but food remains, such as fish-bones and scales, accumulate in the chamber. There are usually 6–7 eggs per clutch and two broods per year. The eggs are short ovate, translucent white like porcelain. One species breeds in central Europe and Br. Is.

Kingfisher* *Alcedo atthis*
Pl. **130**

Site steep banks of rivers and streams where there are plenty of bushes and the soil is sandy or suitable for excavation.

Nest tunnel excavated with the bill, horizontal or slightly sloping upwards, 40 cm to 1 m long, about 5 cm wide, leading to enlarged nest-chamber at the end. No lining material is carried

in, fish remains accumulate.

Eggs 6–7, sometimes 10, short ovate; thin-shelled, translucent white like porcelain. Size 22·6 × 18·7 mm. Weight 4·5 g. Incubation 20–21 days. Usually two broods per year, April–June, occasionally three.

Nestlings no down, pinkish skin; flesh-coloured inside mouth, bluish gape-flanges. Remain in nest for 26–28 days.

BEE-EATERS
Meropidae

A tunnel-type nesting burrow is excavated in a bank of earth, steep or sloping, in open country and not necessarily along a river or stream. The far end of the tunnel is enlarged to form a nest-chamber. No nesting material is taken in but remains of prey, chitinous parts of insects, accumulate in the chamber. There are usually 5–6 eggs per clutch and one brood per year. The eggs are short ovate, translucent white like porcelain. One species breeds regularly in central Europe and occasionally in Br. Is.

Bee-eater* *Merops apiaster*
(Not illustrated)

Site open bushy country where there are banks of earth; the latter may be on a steep-sided sandpit, a cutting for a road or a natural slope in the ground. Several pairs nest close together. (Occasionally in Br. Is.)
Nest horizontal tunnel up to 2 m long and 5 cm wide, is excavated with the bill; nest-chamber at end of tunnel is about 20 cm long. Indigestible parts of insects accumulate but no nesting material is carried in.
Eggs 5–6, sometimes 4 or 7, occasionally 9, short ovate; thin-shelled, translucent white like porcelain. Size 25·6 × 21·8 mm. Weight 6·4 g. Incubation around 24 days. Single brood, May–June.
Nestlings no down, pink skin, pink inside mouth. Remain in nest for about 23–25 days.

ROLLERS
Coraciidae

Rollers nest in natural holes in trees, including Woodpecker-holes, and will use other holes when tree-sites are not available. (Sites include sandy burrows.) Lining material is mostly absent but there may be a few bits of grass and feathers. There are usually 4–5 eggs in a clutch, pure white, and one brood per year. One species breeds in central Europe but not in Br. Is.

Roller *Coracias garrulus*
(Not illustrated)

Site favours holes in trees, including old Woodpecker-holes; also recorded in cliff crevices, banks of sandpits and large nest-boxes. Isolated nests are found in central Europe but examples of colonial breeding occur in southern Europe.
Nest little or no nesting material, debris in the hole usually serves as a lining; sometimes a few bits of grass and feathers, mixed with hair, form a rudimentary nest.
Eggs sometimes 3, usually 4–5; glossy surface, pure white. Size 35·4 × 28·4 mm. Weight 14 g. Incubation 18–19 days. Single brood, late May–June.
Nestlings no down. Remain in nest for about 4 weeks.

HOOPOES   *Upupidae*

Holes of various kinds are used as nest-chambers. These are often in trees, walls and banks, also in nestboxes and even under heaps of stones. Virtually no nest is built, the eggs lie on debris in the cavity, but occasionally a few leaves or twigs are carried in. The eggs are whitish or greenish-grey, stained all over with light brown; clutch-size mostly 4–9. There is usually one brood per year, sometimes two. One species breeds regularly in central Europe and occasionally in Br. Is.

Hoopoe* *Upupa epops*
Pl. **125, 205**

Site any kind of hole, particularly old Woodpecker-holes and other natural holes in old trees; also in banks of earth and old walls, under tree-stumps, wood-stacks and piles of stones, in cowsheds and other old buildings. Nestboxes are also used. (Sporadic breeder in southern England.)

Nest usually no nesting material, occasionally a few sticks or leaves are added to debris in the cavity.

Eggs 4–9; whitish or greenish-grey ground colour becomes so heavily stained that it looks uniform light brown. Size 25·9 × 17·9 mm. Weight around 4 g. Incubation 15–16 days. Usually single brood, May–June, occasionally two broods.

Nestlings long greyish-white down; red inside mouth, yellowish-white gape-flanges. Remain in nest for 20–26 days.

WOODPECKERS   *Picidae*

Holes in trees provide nest-sites for members of this family. Woodpeckers excavate rotting wood but Wryneck uses a natural hole of appropriate size. Signs of excavation, such as wood chips on the ground below a tree, often indicate an occupied hole. No nesting material is taken in; the eggs lie among fine chips of wood and rotting debris at the bottom of the hole. There are usually 5–6 eggs per clutch, pure white, and one brood per year. Eight species breed regularly in central Europe, four of which also breed in Br. Is.

Great Spotted Woodpecker*
Dendrocopos major
(Not illustrated)

Site mature stands of trees, deciduous or evergreen, where some of the wood already shows signs of decay. Also in parks or large gardens with beech, poplar, willow, cherry and pine. Nestholes are mostly 4–8 m from the ground.

Nest excavated hole, circular entrance about 4·6 cm wide; no nesting material carried in, eggs lie on natural debris and fine chips of wood.

Eggs 5–6, sometimes 4 or 8; glossy surface, white. Size 25·8 × 19·0 mm. Weight around 5·4 g. Incubation occasionally 11, generally 12–13 days. Single brood, late April–early June.

Nestlings no down, pinkish-yellow skin. Remain in nest for about 3 weeks.

Middle Spotted Woodpecker
Dendrocopos medius
(Not illustrated)

Site favours deciduous trees, avoids conifers; often in tall specimens of oak, willow and cherry which show signs of decay.

Nest excavated hole, circular entrance about 4 cm wide; no nesting material carried in, eggs lie on natural debris and fine chips of wood.

Eggs generally 5–6, sometimes 4; glossy surface, white. Size 22·6 × 17·9 mm. Weight 4·3 g. Incubation 11–12 days. Single brood, late April–May.

Nestlings no down. Remain in nest for about 3 weeks.

White-backed Woodpecker
Dendrocopos leucotos
(Not illustrated)

Site favours beech, birch and elm trees which show signs of decay; locally in conifers.

Nest excavated hole is about 6 cm long and 4·9–5·1 cm wide; no nesting material carried in, eggs lie on natural debris and fine chips of wood.

Eggs 3–5; glossy surface, white. Size 28·1 × 20·4 mm. Weight 6·7 g. Incubation period not known. Single brood, late April–May.

Nestlings no information available.

Lesser Spotted Woodpecker*
Dendrocopos minor
(Not illustrated)

Site favours decaying deciduous trees, particularly rotting specimens of willow, poplar and birch; also dead branches of fruit trees. Nest-holes are mostly 3–6 m from the ground, some are higher.

Nest excavated hole, nearly circular entrance, 3·2 cm wide; no nesting material carried in, eggs lie on natural debris and fine chips of wood.

Eggs 5–6; glossy surface, white. Size 18·7 × 14·4 mm. Weight 3 g. Incubation about 14 days. Single brood, late April–June.

Nestlings no down, pink skin. Remain in nest for 18 days.

Three-toed Woodpecker
Picoides tridactylus
(Not illustrated)

Site decaying specimens of spruce, silver fir and birch in the far north.

Nest excavated hole, circular entrance about 5 cm wide; no nesting material carried in, eggs lie on natural debris and fine chips of wood.

Eggs 4–5; glossy surface, white. Size 24·8 × 18·0 mm. Weight 4·6 g. Very little known about incubation period. Single brood, late May–early June.

Nestlings no information available.

Green Woodpecker* *Picus viridis*
(Not illustrated)

Site open type of deciduous woodland, copses or farmland, parkland with scattered trees and orchards. Nest-holes are often in beech, alder, oak, poplar and decaying fruit trees.

Nest excavated hole, circular entrance about 6·5 cm wide; no nesting material carried in, eggs lie on natural debris and fine chips of wood.

Eggs 5–7, less often 8; glossy surface, white. Size 30·9 × 22·9 mm. Weight around 7·9–8·1 g. Incubation 15–16, occasionally 17 days. Single brood, April/May–June.

Nestlings no down, dark pink skin. Remain in nest for about 27 days.

Grey-headed Woodpecker
Picus canus
Pl. **126**

Site open type of deciduous woodland and large orchards with decaying trees; avoids conifers.

Nest excavated hole; circular entrance about 6 cm wide but the total excavation may be 30 cm deep and 18 cm wide.

Eggs sometimes 5, usually 6–7; glossy surface, white. Size 27·7 × 20·4 mm. Weight 6·5 g. Incubation about 14–16 days. Single brood, May–mid-June.

Nestlings remain in nest for about 26–28 days.

Black Woodpecker *Dryocopus martius*
(Not illustrated)

Site high up in mature trees of pine, spruce, beech and oak; not necessarily in decaying wood. Nest-hole is often in a tree somewhat isolated from the others and which has comparatively few branches. The majority of holes are 7–10 m from the ground.

Nest excavated hole, shape of entrance long-ovate and about 10 cm wide; no nesting material carried in, eggs lie on natural debris and fine chips of wood. (Roosting holes are also excavated.)

Eggs 3–4, less often 6; glossy surface, white. Size 34·9 × 25·9 mm. Weight around 11·5–12·3 g. Incubation 12–14 days. Single brood, mid-April–mid-May.

Nestlings remain in nest for about 26 days.

Wryneck* *Jynx torquilla*
(Not illustrated)

Site favours old Woodpecker-holes and natural holes in trees, also occupies nestboxes; occasionally in hole of wall. Does not excavate its own hole but will eject other species occupying site, destroying the eggs or young and removing the nesting material.

Nest no excavation, usually no nesting material although sometimes a little material is left behind after an occupant has been evicted.

Eggs 7–10, occasionally 12; glossy surface, white. Size 20·8 × 15·4 mm. Weight around 2·0 g. Incubation generally 13–14 days, sometimes 12. Usually single brood, May–June, but sometimes two broods per year. Replacement clutch.

Nestlings no down, pink skin. Remain in nest 23–26 days, according to Henze.

LARKS

Nests are of simple construction, small cups of grass and fibrous rootlets, built in a slight hollow in the ground and well-hidden by tufts of grass or other low cover. The eggs are mostly whitish, speckled and spotted with dark markings. There are usually 3–5 eggs in a clutch and two broods per year. Three species breed in central Europe, two in Br. Is.

Crested Lark *Galerida cristata*
Pl. **132**
Site arid country, including fields and farm tracks, roadside verges and waste ground with heaps of rubble. Nest hidden in low cover, built in a depression on the ground.
Nest looks carelessly built, made out of grass and rootlets, lined with finer grass.
Eggs 3–5, less often 6; whitish ground colour, spotted and speckled with yellowish-brown and grey, giving a marbled effect. Size 22·7 × 16·8 mm. Weight 3·2 g. Incubation 12–13 days. Two broods, late April–June. Replacement clutch. Rare Cuckoo-host.
Nestlings yellow down; yellow inside mouth, sometimes with dark spots on tongue, yellow gape-flanges. Remain in nest for 9–10 days.

Skylark* *Alauda arvensis*
Pl. **134, 181, 251**
Site open ground, cultivated or waste, often in grass or among growing crops. Nest hidden in low cover, built in depression in the ground.
Nest rather flat and untidy on the outside, smooth and rounded on the inside; made out of grass and rootlets, lined with finer grass.

Eggs 3–5; ground colour varies from whitish-grey to yellowish or reddish, closely spotted with brown, often densely marked at blunt end. Size 24·1 × 16·8 mm. Weight 3·4 g. Incubation sometimes 11–12 days, generally 14. Mostly two broods March/April–July, sometimes three per year. Replacement clutch. Cuckoo-host from time to time.
Nestlings scanty yellow down, blackish skin; yellow inside mouth, sometimes with black spots on tongue, yellow gape-flanges. Remain in nest for 9–10 days.

Woodlark* *Lullula arborea*
Pl. **133, 182**
Site not as open as previous species, trees or bushes are usually in the vicinity. Favours uncultivated verges of woods or felled clearings with low ground cover; also among heather near conifers or on heathland.
Nest more substantial than previous species, about 10 cm wide, built with a deeper depression, made out of grass and moss, lined with finer grass and hair.
Eggs 3–4, sometimes 5; whitish ground colour (sometimes with reddish tinge), speckled reddish-brown or olive-brown, densely marked at blunt end. Size 21·6 ×

16·3 mm. Weight 2·7 g. Incubation 13–15 days. Mostly two broods, late March–July, sometimes three per year. Replacement clutch. Cuckoo-host from time to time.

Nestlings yellowish-brown down on upperparts; pinkish-yellow inside mouth, three black spots on tongue, pale yellow gape-flanges. Remain in nest for 9–10 days.

SWALLOWS AND MARTINS   *Hirundinidae*

Swallows build an open bowl-type nest on a ledge inside a building, usually in a shed or outhouse. House Martin builds an enclosed nest, with an entrance-hole at the top, against the outside wall of a building, usually under the eaves; nests are in colonies. Sand Martin, also a colonial breeder, tunnels into the walls of a sandpit or embankment of some kind. Crag Martin builds a Swallow-type nest against a rock-face. Nests are made with mud except for Sand Martin. Eggs of all species are white, with or without markings. House Martin and Sand Martin are unmarked. Swallow and Crag Martin are marked with reddish-brown spots and grey shell-marks. There are usually 4–5 eggs per clutch and two broods per year, except for Crag Martin which is single-brooded. Four species breed in central Europe, three in Br. Is.

Swallow* *Hirundo rustica*
Pl. **127**

Site inside a building with free access and some kind of rafter or ledge on which to build the nest. Often inside farm buildings, also in house porches and garages, even inside a living-room where a window is kept permanently open.

Nest shallow bowl or saucer, open above; made out of damp mud and straw or grass, mixed with hair and feathers; smooth on the inside, a few feathers provide a soft lining.

Eggs 4–5, sometimes 6; white ground colour with grey shell-marks and reddish-brown spots. Size 19·3 × 13·5 mm. Weight around 2 g. Incubation 14–16, less commonly 18 days. Usually two broods, sometimes three, April/May–August/September.

Nestlings scanty grey down, pale yellow inside mouth, whitish gape-flanges. Remain in nest for about 3 weeks.

House Martin* *Delichon urbica*
Pl. **128**

Site on the outside of a building, frequently with overhang of eaves, also under window-sills or outside ledges. Sociable breeder, nests are often close together or even one on top of another. Colonies often nest against rock-faces south of the Alps.

Nest enclosed type of bowl with entrance-hole, about 4 cm wide, at the top; made out of mud and grass, plastered against a wall under an overhang, lined with a few feathers.

Eggs 4–5; white, unmarked (the eggs illustrated in Plate 128 look as though they are finely spotted;

this is due to excrement from flies or parasites). Size 18·3 × 13·2 mm. Weight around 1·4–1·6 g. Incubation 14–15 days. Usually two broods, sometimes three, May–August/September.

Nestlings greyish-white down; dark yellow inside mouth, pale yellow gape-flanges. Remain in nest for 19–22 days.

Sand Martin* *Riparia riparia*
Pl. **129**

Site steep side of sandpit or gravelpit, bank of loose earth suitable for tunnelling, occasionally in drainpipe or wall. Nests in colonies.

Nest horizontal tunnel 4–6 cm wide, excavated with bill and feet, widened at the end into a nest-chamber; tunnels are mostly 60–80 cm long, up to 100 cm. Nesting material consists of bits of straw and feathers.

Eggs 5–6; uniform white. Size 17·4 × 12·7 mm. Weight around 1·5 g. Incubation 12–16 days. Two broods, May–July.

Nestlings sparse grey down on head and back, otherwise naked; pale yellow inside mouth, whitish gape-flanges. Remain in nest for 16–22 days.

Crag Martin *Ptyonoprogne rupestris*
Pl. **161**

Site steep rock-face, protected from above, in a fissure or inside a cave.

Nest open bowl type, similar to Swallow; mud and grass plastered against rock-face and lined with finer grass, hair and feathers.

Eggs 4–5; white ground colour marked with lots of small grey and reddish-brown spots; less densely marked than Swallow. Size 20·1 × 14·0 mm. Incubation about 14 days, according to Prenn. Probably a single brood, mid-May–July.

Nestlings remain in nest for 25–26 days, according to Prenn.

ORIOLES   *Oriolidae*

One species breeds regularly in central Europe and irregularly in Br. Is. Golden Oriole builds a hammock type of nest which is slung in the angle of a fork between two horizontal branches, in the outer edge of the crown of a deciduous tree. The eggs are pinkish-white, sparsely marked with dark spots. There are usually 3 eggs per clutch and one brood per year.

Golden Oriole* *Oriolus oriolus*
Pl. **110**

Site trees in parks, orchards, large gardens, along river banks and in woodland. Frequently in apple, chestnut, beech, birch and oak, rarely in conifer. Nests are high up in the outer branches, built in the angle of a fork between two horizontal branches. (Not a regular breeder in Br. Is.)

Nest closely woven structure,

made out of fine bits of grass, bark fibre, moss, wool, flower-heads and feathers. Sometimes bits of paper are incorporated.

Eggs 3–5; pinkish-white ground colour, sparsely marked with purplish-brown or blackish spots.

Size 30·8 × 21·3 mm. Weight around 7 g. Incubation 14–15 days. Single brood, late May–June. Replacement clutch.

Nestlings short yellow down; reddish-orange inside mouth. Remain in nest for 14–15 days.

CROWS   *Corvidae*

As well as the typical Crows (*Corvus* species) this family includes Magpie, Nutcracker, Jay and two species of Chough. Some are solitary, others are colonial breeders. Nests are built out of sticks or twigs lined with softer material. Sites include trees, rock fissures and holes. The eggs are pale grey or greenish-blue with dark markings, except for the two species of Chough which have dark markings on a cream or white ground colour. There are mostly 4–6 eggs per clutch and one brood per year. Ten members of the Crow family breed in central Europe, eight in Br. Is.

Raven* *Corvus corax*
Pl. **63**

Site ledges and crevices in steep cliffs overlooking the sea or inland on moors and mountains; nests are also built in trees, mostly at a height of 8–25 m from the ground.

Nest solidly built out of sticks and twigs mixed with earth and roots; neatly lined inside to a depth of 5 cm with softer material, often bits of bark, moss, leaves and animal hair. Old nests are frequently used as a foundation in the following year.

Eggs 4–7; pale greenish-blue ground colour marked with light and dark olive-brown spots and blotches, sometimes with grey shell-marks. Size 49·7 × 33·4 mm. Weight 33 g. Incubation 20–21, more rarely 22 days. Single brood, late February–April. Replacement clutch.

Nestlings sparse down, later down-feathers also sparse; red inside mouth. Remains in nest for about 40 days.

Carrion Crow* *Corvus corone corone*
Pl. **64**

Site tall trees, deciduous or conifer, and cliffs. Nests are solitary, usually 8–12 m up the tree but some are lower down.

Nest bowl at least 50 cm wide; built out of sticks and twigs, mixed with earth and roots, lined with bits of bark and animal hair. *Eggs* 4–6; pale greenish-blue ground colour with dark brown or olive-brown spots and blotches, and grey shell-marks. Size 43·5 × 30·1 mm. Weight around 19 g. Incubation 17–19 days. Single brood, March–May. Replacement clutch.

Nestlings pink skin, sparse down;

red inside mouth, narrow gape-flanges are yellow. Remain in nest for 30–32, sometimes 35 days.

Hooded Crow* *Corvus corone cornix*
(Not illustrated)

Site similar to Carrion Crow but also in low bushes. Nests are solitary. (In Br. Is. mainly confined to northern areas.)

Nest similar to Carrion Crow.

Eggs 5–6; pale greenish-blue ground colour with dark brown or olive-brown spots and blotches, sometimes also with grey shell-marks. Size, weight and incubation similar to Carrion Crow. Single brood, April–May.

Nestlings similar to Carrion Crow.

Rook* *Corvus frugilegus*
Pl. **65, 215**

Site tall trees, deciduous or conifer, in the outer branches of the crown. There are often several nests in the same tree and colonies are usually large.

Nest construction similar to Carrion Crow but smaller and not so deep.

Eggs 4–5, sometimes 6; pale bluish-green ground colour heavily marked with dark brown or olive-brown spots and blotches. Size 41·0 × 28·3 mm. Weight around 16 g. Incubation 16–18 days. Single brood, March–April/May.

Nestlings brownish skin, sparse down on back; red inside mouth, pale yellow gape-flanges. Remain in nest for about 30 days.

Jackdaw* *Corvus monedula*
Pl. **67**

Site holes and crevices in trees, chimneys, ruined buildings, church towers, quarries and cliffs. Nests are in colonies.

Nest sticks and straw mixed with earth and fibrous material, lined with finer twigs, animal wool and bits of rubbish.

Eggs 5–6; pale bluish-green ground colour, less heavily marked than other species; grey-brown or blue-brown spots are more concentrated at the blunt end. Size 33·7 × 25·2 mm. Weight 12 g. Incubation 17–18 days. Single brood, April–May. Replacements only during normal laying period.

Nestlings pale pink skin, sparse down on back; red inside mouth, yellow gape-flanges. Remain in nest for 30–35 days.

Magpie* *Pica pica*
Pl. **66**

Site tall trees, deciduous or conifer, untrimmed hedgerows and thorn bushes. The nest may be high up in the outer branches of the tree canopy or comparatively low in a thorny thicket.

Nest domed with side entrance; built of sticks and thorny twigs, lined with earth and fine rootlets.

Eggs 5–7, occasionally 8; ground colour varies from greenish-blue to yellowish or greenish-grey, densely marked with grey and brown spots. Size 34·1 × 24·2 mm. Weight 8–10 g. Incubation 17–18 days. Single brood, March/April–May/June. Replacement clutch.

Nestlings yellowish skin, no down; red inside mouth, yellow gape-flanges. Remain in nest for 25–27 days.

Nutcracker *Nucifraga caryocatactes*
Pl. **214**

Site dense conifer plantations. Nest is built close to the trunk, on a bare branch mostly at a height of 4–7 m from the ground.
Nest deep bowl of twigs and lichen, lined with a felted layer of moss, humus and fine grass.
Eggs 3–4; very pale bluish-green ground colour, evenly marked with grey and olive-brown flecks. Size 33·9 × 24·9 mm. Weight 11 g. Incubation 16–18 days. Single brood, March–April.
Nestlings remain in nest for about 22 days.

Jay* *Garrulus glandarius*
Pl. **68, 256**

Site at varying heights in bushes and trees. Most nests are 2–5 m from the ground. Favours deciduous woodland with shrub layer in Br. Is., but on the Continent also nests in more open conifer forests, from the plains to the mountains. Nests are built close to the tree-trunk.
Nest sticks and twigs form a comparatively shallow bowl, lined with rootlets.
Eggs 5–6, less often 7; greenish-grey or olive-brown ground colour, finely mottled with darker brown, particularly at the blunt end where there may also be black hair-lines. Size 31·6 ×

23·0 mm. Weight 8 g. Incubation 16–17 days. Single brood, April–June. Nests are easily deserted if disturbed.
Nestlings pink skin, no down; pale pink inside mouth and gape-flanges. Remain in nest for 19–20, less commonly 22 days.

Chough* *Pyrrhocorax pyrrhocorax*
Pl. **216**

Site rock crevice or ledge of cliff overlooking the sea, also inland on mountains, rock-faces, in quarries and old ruins. (Only a few colonies still exist in Br. Is., none in English counties.)
Nest made out of sticks and twigs, stems of local plants such as heather, and lined with grass, hair or wool.
Eggs 3–5; creamy ground colour with brownish spots and oblong flecks. Size 39·4 × 27·9 mm. Weight around 13 g. Incubation 19–21 days. Single brood, April–May/June.
Nestlings sparse greyish-brown down; pink inside mouth, yellow gape-flanges. Remain in nest for about 38 days.

Alpine Chough *Pyrrhocorax graculus*
Pl. **217**

Site inaccessible rock ledges and crevices in the mountains, less frequently in ruined building or tower. Sometimes nests in colonies.
Nest made out of dry branches and rootlets, lined with grass and hair; seeding heads of plants may also be incorporated.

Eggs 4–5; whitish or pale green ground colour, marked with blotches, spots and oblongs in olive-brown and grey. Size 37·2 × 25·9 mm. Incubation 18–21 days. Single brood, May–June. *Nestlings* remain in nest for 31 days.

TITS   *Paridae*

Members of this family nest in holes, usually in trees or nest-boxes, rarely higher than 4 m from the ground. Moss forms the bulk of the nesting material. The eggs are white with reddish-brown spots. Clutch-size usually 7–10 eggs. There are two broods per year, except for Marsh Tit which only has one brood and Willow Tit which is probably single-brooded. Six species breed in central Europe and in Br. Is.

Great Tit* *Parus major*
Pl. **121**

Site favours holes in trees, uses nestboxes readily and will also nest in a variety of holes including drainpipes, letterboxes, holes in walls and banks of earth. *Nest* foundation layer of moss several centimetres thick, typical of all the Tit family; on top of this is more moss, mixed with bents, rootlets and bark fibres, felted with animal hair or plant down. *Eggs* sometimes 6, usually 7–10, but also up to 13; white ground colour with reddish-brown spots. The size and number of spots varies and some eggs are almost pure white according to Makatsch. Size 17·3 × 13·5 mm. Weight 1·6 g. Incubation 13–14 days. Two broods, April–July, occasionally three. *Nestlings* yellowish-pink skin, grey down on head only; yellow inside mouth, pale yellow gape-flanges. Remain in nest for 15–18, less frequently 20, days.

Coal Tit* *Parus ater*
Pl. **150**

Site similar to Great Tit, a hole of almost any kind, including nest-boxes. Shows some preference for holes at ground level, sites include mouse runs and rabbit burrows. *Nest* similar to Great Tit; lining often has plenty of animal hair, rabbit or hare. *Eggs* 7–8, often 9–10, occasionally more; white ground colour, finely spotted with reddish-brown markings which are sometimes concentrated at the blunt end. Size 14·7 × 11·6 mm. Weight around 1·4 g. Incubation 14–16 days. Two broods, April–June. Replacement clutch. *Nestlings* long grey down on head, otherwise no down; yellow inside mouth, pale yellow gape-flanges. Remain in nest for 16–17 days.

Blue Tit* *Parus caeruleus*
Pl. **122, 148**

Site similar to Great Tit, a hole of almost any kind, mostly at a height of 2–4 m from the ground. Uses nestboxes readily.

Nest similar to Great Tit.

Eggs 10–13 (clutch-size varies, may be higher or lower); white ground colour with reddish-brown spots. Slightly smaller but otherwise similar to Great Tit, difficult to distinguish from Marsh Tit and Coal Tit. Size 15·4 × 11·9 mm. Weight around 1·2–1·3 g. Incubation 13–15 days. Two broods, April–July.

Nestlings pink skin, sparse down on head; dull yellow inside mouth, very pale yellow gape-flanges. Remain in nest for 17–20 days.

Marsh Tit* *Parus palustris*
Pl. **124**

Site natural holes or crevices in trees and rotting tree-stumps, showing a preference for those with a narrow entrance. Seldom uses a hole in the ground; recorded in nestboxes but apparently uses them less readily than Great Tit and Blue Tit.

Nest similar to Great Tit.

Eggs 7–9, sometimes 10; similar to Blue Tit and Coal Tit. Size 16·1 × 12·2 mm. Weight 1 g. Incubation 14 days. Single brood, late April–May/June.

Nestlings brownish-grey down on head only; brilliant yellow inside mouth, pale yellow gape-flanges. Remain in nest for 17–19 days.

Willow Tit* *Parus montanus*
Pl. **151**

Site rotting wood, suitable for excavating into nest-hole, often in dead tree-trunk or stump.

Entrance-hole is oval, not circular; chips lying on the ground often indicate occupied site above.

Nest unlike other members of the family, this species rarely uses moss and then only very little. The foundation layer is made up of wood chips and fibrous material, with the usual animal hair or seeding heads added as lining.

Eggs 7–8, sometimes 6 or 10; whitish ground colour with reddish spots, markings more concentrated at the blunt end, difficult to distinguish from Marsh Tit. Size 15·6 × 12·2 mm. Weight around 1 g. Incubation 13 days. Probably a single brood, April–May/June.

Nestlings brownish-grey down on head only; yellow inside mouth, pale yellow-gape flanges. Remain in nest for 16–19 days.

Crested Tit* *Parus cristatus*
Pl. **123, 149**

Site at varying heights in decaying tree-trunks or stumps in conifer forests. Frequently in natural holes and old Woodpecker-holes but also in squirrels' dreys, old nest of birds of prey, piles of wood on the ground, and in nestboxes. (In Br. Is. confined to Scottish Highlands.)

Nest large amount of moss mixed with fibrous material and animal hair; the rim is sometimes decorated with spider's webs.

Eggs 5–7, up to 10 also recorded; whitish ground colour and bold reddish-brown spots which are concentrated at one end. Size 16·0 × 12·4 mm. Weight 1·3 g.

Incubation 15–18 days. Two broods, April–June. *Nestlings* yellowish-pink skin, no down except for brownish-grey tuft on head; dull yellow inside mouth, pale yellow-gape-flanges. Remain in nest for about 19 days.

PENDULINE TITS   *Remizidae*

One species breeds in central Europe but not in Br. Is. The nest and eggs of Penduline Tit are quite different from those of the typical Tits (*Paridae*). The nest is suspended from the outer branches of a bush or tree, on marshy ground, often overhanging water. The eggs are creamy-white and unmarked. There are usually 7–8 eggs per clutch and two broods per year.

Penduline Tit *Remiz pendulinus*
(Not illustrated)

Site favours outer branches of a bush or tree overhanging the water; often in poplars and willows, also locally in reeds. Nests are mostly at heights of 3–8 m.

Nest oval shape, about 15 cm long and 9 cm wide, with a tunnel entrance at the side; carefully woven structure, enclosing the tips of outer branches, making a hanging nest. Material includes bark fibres, long stems and seed-ing heads of poplar and willow, lined with more plant down and felted with hair or fur.

Eggs 5–8, occasionally up to 10; creamy-white and unmarked. Size 16·3 × 10·8 mm. Weight 0·9–1·0 g. Incubation 12–14 days. Two broods, late April–June, sometimes three. Males are polygamous and mate with a second female during incubation. *Nestlings* no down; orange-red inside mouth, broad gape-flanges which are yellow. Remain in nest for 15–16 days, sometimes longer.

LONG-TAILED TITS   *Aegithalidae*

One species breeds in central Europe and Br. Is. The nest is an oval-shaped ball of moss, thick-walled and decorated on the outside with lichen, with a side-entrance towards the top. Nests are often in forks of trees or in thorny thickets of gorse, briar or bramble. There are mostly 7–11 eggs per clutch, dull white with fine reddish-brown spots, and two broods per year.

Long-tailed Tit* *Aegithalos caudatus*
Pl. **147**

Site often in fork of tree but also in branches further from the trunk, usually in deciduous species or in thorny thickets of gorse, briar or bramble. Height from the ground varies, frequently 1–12 m but also up to 20 m.

Nest oval-shaped structure with

a side-entrance; made out of moss, cobwebs and hair, decorated with lichen on the outside and lined with lots of feathers. Blends well with the surroundings and is easily missed.

Eggs 7–11, 6 or 12 also known; dull white ground colour with zone of fine reddish-brown spots; some markings are so faint that eggs appear almost uniform white. Size 13·6 × 10·9 mm. Weight 0·94 g. Incubation 12–13 days. Two broods, mid-March–early June. Replacement clutch.

Nestlings no down, pink skin; yellow inside mouth (turning orange later), whitish gape-flanges. Remain in nest for 15–16 days.

TREECREEPERS   *Certhiidae*

Treecreepers nest in some kind of crevice, often behind rotting bark on a tree or in the crack of a wooden shed, less frequently in wall-crevices. Twigs, fibres, moss, hair and feathers are carried into the crevice through a mere slit at the entrance. The eggs are similar to those of the typical Tits (*Paridae*): white with reddish-brown spots. Clutches usually have 5–6 eggs and there are two broods per year. Two species breed in central Europe; one species breeds widely in Br. Is. and breeding of the other (Short-toed) has been confirmed in one locality in Dorset.

Treecreeper* *Certhia familiaris*
Pl. **152**

Site behind rotting bark on tree-trunks, also in decaying holes of branches and crevices in wooden sheds; less frequently in cracks of buildings and occasionally in stacked wood. Uses nestboxes. Nest-sites are mostly 1–4 m from the ground.

Nest crevice stuffed with material which includes small twigs, moss, plant down, animal hair and feathers.

Eggs 5–6, sometimes 7; whitish ground colour with reddish-brown markings which vary from fine spots to larger flecks, often forming a ring at the blunt end. Size 15·9 × 12·2 mm. Weight around 1·1 g. Incubation 13–15 days. Two broods, April–July.

Liable to desert if disturbed during the early stages.

Nestlings pink skin, no down except yellowish-grey tuft on head; orange inside mouth, yellowish gape-flanges. Remain in nest for 16–17 days.

Short-toed Treecreeper*
Certhia brachydactyla
Pl. **120**

Site similar to previous species, crevices and holes, including nestboxes. Nest-sites are mostly 2–4 m from the ground. (One breeding record confirmed in Dorset, others suspected but identification from previous species makes confirmation difficult.)

Nest similar to previous species.

Eggs occasionally 4, usually 5–7,

sometimes more; whitish ground colour with reddish-brown spots, often forming a ring at the end. The spots are more clearly defined and coarser than in previous species. Size 16·1 × 12·1 mm. Weight 1·1 g. Incubation around 15 days. Two broods per year, April–July. Liable to desert if disturbed during the early stages.

Nestlings pink skin, no down except brownish-grey tuft on head; orange inside mouth, pale yellow gape-flanges. Remain in nest for about 16 days.

NUTHATCHES   *Sittidae*

One species breeds in central Europe and in Br. Is. Nests are in natural holes in trees, old Woodpecker-holes and nestboxes. The size of the entrance-hole is reduced by plastering it with mud. Nesting material in the hole consists mainly of bark fibres. The eggs are similar to the typical Tits (*Paridae*): white with fine reddish-brown spots. There are usually 6–8 eggs per clutch and one brood per year.

Nuthatch* *Sitta europaea*
Pl. **118**

Site holes in trees, often in old Woodpecker-holes, also in nestboxes and only occasionally in a wall. Sites in trees may be at a considerable height. Holes too large are reduced to size by plastering mud round entrance.

Nest bark fibres and dead leaves are loosely arranged in the hole; these are pulled over the eggs before the bird leaves.

Eggs 6–8, less often 9; milky white ground colour marked with reddish-brown spots, zoned at the blunt end, and a few purplish-grey shell-marks (reminiscent of Great Tit but larger). Size 19·9 × 14·6 mm. Weight around 2·2 g. Incubation 15 days. Usually single-brooded, April–May.

Nestlings sparse yellowish-grey down, pink skin; lemon-yellow inside mouth, very pale gape-flanges. Remain in nest for about 22–24 days.

WALLCREEPERS   *Tichodromadidae*

One species breeds in central Europe, none in Br. Is. Nests are mostly in crevices of inaccessible rock-faces at high altitudes. Nesting material consists of lichen, moss and grass. The eggs are long ovate, white, sparsely marked with fine reddish-brown spots. There are usually 4–5 eggs per clutch and one brood per year.

Wallcreeper *Tichodroma muraria*
Pl. **119**

Site favours deep crevices of inaccessible rock-faces, particularly with mountain streams in the vicinity; occasionally in old walls at lower altitudes.

Nest loosely arranged with plenty

of moss, lichen, rootlets, grass, bits of animal wool and soft seeding heads of plants; felted lining includes animal hair (mouse, hare, chamois) and sometimes feathers.

Eggs sometimes 3, generally 4–5, long ovate; milky white ground colour, sparsely marked with small reddish-brown spots; markings mostly concentrated at the blunt end. Size 21·3 × 14·3 mm. Incubation 18–19 days. Single brood, May–June.

Nestlings remain in nest for about 26 days.

BABBLERS   *Timaliidae*

Bearded Reedling, previously known as Bearded Tit, is the only species of Babbler to breed in central Europe, also in Br. Is. Nests are made out of old stems of reeds and sedge, lined with flowering panicles, in extensive reedbeds. The eggs are creamy white with blackish-brown flecks. There are usually 5–7 eggs per clutch and two broods per year.

Bearded Reedling (Tit)*
Panurus biarmicus
Pl. **153**

Site extensive reedbeds where there is little chance of disturbance. Nests are usually low down in old stems of reed or sedge, close to the water's edge. (East Anglia and a few other localities.)

Nest broken and dead stems from previous year's growth of reed and sedge form the foundation for a comparatively deep bowl, open-type structure; this is lined with finer bits and flowering panicles of rush, sedge and reed, grass and a few feathers.

Eggs 5–7, occasionally 4; creamy white ground colour with blackish-brown flecks and streaks. Size 18·4 × 14·1 mm. Incubation 12–13 days. Two broods, April–July.

Nestlings no down; red inside mouth, black tongue with white projections, yellow gape-flanges. Remain in nest for about 15–16 days.

DIPPERS   *Cinclidae*

One species breeds in central Europe and in Br. Is. Dippers nest along hill streams where the water runs swiftly over boulders and stones. The nest is domed with a side-entrance, built into a crevice of some kind along the banks, often between boulders or on a ledge under a bridge. The eggs are pure white. There are usually 4–6 eggs per clutch and two broods per year.

Dipper* *Cinclus cinclus*
(Not illustrated)
Site near shallow streams of clear water, running swiftly over boul-

ders and stones, in hilly country. Nests may be along the bank, between tree-roots or boulders, in a rock crevice behind a waterfall, or on a ledge, under a bridge. *Nest* domed structure made out of moss, with round entrance-hole at the side, lined with dead leaves and bits of grass. *Eggs* 4–6; pure white. Size 25·1 × 18·5 mm. Weight around 4·8 g. Incubation 15–16, less

often 17, days. Two broods, March/April–June/July. *Nestlings* scanty bluish-grey down on head and back; pale pink inside mouth, broad gape-flanges which are yellow. Remain in nest for 19–20 days, occasionally for only 18 days.

WRENS   *Troglodytidae*

One species breeds in central Europe and in Br. Is. Wrens build domed or rounded nests of moss, with a circular entrance-hole at the side, in a variety of crevices or holes. Nests are nearly always in low cover but sites include nestboxes and garden sheds. There are usually 5–6 eggs, white with brick-red spots, and two broods per year.

Wren* *Troglodytes troglodytes*
Pl. **154**

Site rotting tree-stumps, ivy-clad walls or fences, among brambles or piles of brushwood in almost any kind of hole or crevice. Many nests are in low cover, up to about 50 cm height from the ground. Nestboxes and sites inside sheds or outhouses may be higher.

Nest circular or domed, with a rounded entrance-hole at the side; made out of plenty of moss mixed with leaves, bits of bracken, grass or straw and lined with lots of feathers. The male

builds more than one nest but the female selects one, lining it with feathers; unlined nests are not used for rearing young.

Eggs 5–7; white ground colour with fine reddish-brown spots. Size 16·1 × 12·0 mm. Weight around 1·3 g. Incubation 14–16 days. Two broods, April–July. Males mate with a second or even a third female during the breeding season. Frequent Cuckoo-host.

Nestlings scanty greyish-black down; dark yellow inside mouth, paler gape-flanges. Remain in nest for 16–17 days.

THRUSHES   *Turdidae*

As well as the typical Thrushes (*Turdus* species) a number of other birds are often included in this family: Nightingale, Bluethroat, Robin, Redstart, Wheatear, Stonechat, Whinchat and Rock Thrush. Nest-sites vary from natural hollows at ground level or just above it in some kind of hole or low cover (Nightingale, Bluethroat, Robin, Wheatear, Stonechat, Whinchat, Redwing and Rock Thrush) to holes higher up in trees and buildings (Redstart); there are also comparatively substantial nests in bushes and trees (Blackbird, Song Thrush, Mistle Thrush, Redwing and Fieldfare). Nesting material includes twigs, leaves, moss and animal hair; the outer layer may be solidified by plastering it with mud from the inside (typical of many Song Thrush nests) and there may also be an inner lining – added to the plastered mud – of grass or soft material (typical of many Blackbird nests). Fieldfares nest in colonies, other species nest singly.

Key to eggs: uniform olive-brown (Nightingale); uniform pale blue (Wheatear); uniform blue-green (Redstart); whitish with reddish markings (Robin); blue-green with reddish markings (Whinchat, Blackbird, Ring Ouzel); grey-green with reddish markings (Stonechat); blue with a few black spots (Song Thrush); pale blue ground (or rufous) with irregular pattern of bold reddish markings (Mistle Thrush). Clutch-size mostly 4–6 eggs; one to two broods per year. Seventeen members of this family breed in central Europe; eleven of these breed regularly in Br. Is., others only sporadically or very locally, and two species (Thrush Nightingale, Rock Thrush) have never bred.

Nightingale* *Luscinia megarhynchos*
Pl. **76**

Site well-hidden in cover at ground level or just above, often in brambles or nettles; occasionally in branches of young trees, up to about 80 cm from the ground.

Nest loosely built but comparatively deep; made out of dead leaves, grass, rootlets, moss and hair.

Eggs 4–6; glossy olive-brown appearance. Size 21·0 × 15·6 mm. Weight from 2·3–3·0 g. Incubation 13, less frequently 14, days. Usually single-brooded, early May–June, but two broods are a possibility. Replacement clutch. Cuckoo-host from time to time.

Nestlings pink skin, long blackish-brown down on head and back; dark yellow inside mouth. Remain in nest for 11–12 days.

Thrush Nightingale *Luscinia luscinia*
Pl. **186**

Site between old mossy tree-roots, often on swampy ground with tangled growth.

Nest similar to Nightingale.

Eggs 4–6; light blue ground colour overlaid with olive-brown (almost uniform olive-brown in appearance). Size 21·7 × 16·2 mm. Weight around 3 g. Incubation 13 days. Usually single-brooded, May–June.

Nestlings pale pink skin, sparse greyish-blue down on head and back; yellow inside mouth. Remain in nest for about 10 days.

White-spotted Bluethroat
Luscinia svecica cyanecula
Pl. **78, 187**

Site natural hollow under grass tuft or just above ground level in thickets of willow or similar scrub growth on marshy ground.

Nest made out of leaves, stalks and rootlets, lined with fine bents, hair and plant down.
Eggs 5–6; greenish-grey ground colour, densely marked with fine reddish-brown speckles. Size 18·9 × 14·2 mm. Weight 2 g. Incubation 13 days. Usually single-brooded, late April–May.
Nestlings dark grey down, orange inside mouth, whitish-yellow flanges. Remain in nest for about 13 days.

Red-spotted Bluethroat*
Luscinia svecica svecica
(Not illustrated)
Site similar to previous species, marshy thickets and heaths, well-hidden at ground level or just above. (Nested Scotland in 1968.)
Nest similar to previous species.
Eggs generally 5–6, sometimes 4; greenish-blue ground colour, densely marked with fine reddish-brown speckles as in previous species. Size 18·5 × 14·0 mm. Weight around 2 g. Incubation 13, less frequently 14 days. Usually single-brooded, June, occasionally a second brood in July.
Nestlings remain in nest for about 13 days.

Robin* *Erithacus rubecula*
Pl. **77** (nest with Cuckoo's egg)
Site in a hollow on sloping ground, hidden by some form of ground cover, and in various holes including rotting tree-stumps, among ivy on walls, inside discarded tins, usually at ground level or just above but occasionally higher. Uses open-type nestboxes.

Nest foundation of dead leaves and moss, lined with fine bents, rootlets, fibres, animal hair and plant down.
Eggs 5–7; whitish ground colour with reddish-brown speckles and blotches. Size 19·4 × 14·8 mm. Weight 2 g. Incubation 13–14 days. Two broods, March/April–July. Frequent Cuckoo-host (see Pl. 77).
Nestlings tufts of blackish down on head and back; dark yellow inside mouth and gape-flanges. Remain in nest for 12–14, occasionally 15 days.

Redstart* *Phoenicurus phoenicurus*
Pl. **71**
Site at varying heights in a hole or crevice of some kind; often in old trees, particularly pollard willow, also in stacks of cordwood, discarded tins, holes in walls and nestboxes. Rarely in ruined buildings.
Nest loosely made out of dry leaves, grass and rootlets, lined with hair and plenty of feathers.
Eggs 5–7, less often 8; uniform, pale blue-green. Size 18·7 × 13·8 mm. Weight around 2 g. Incubation 13–14 days. Two broods, May–July. Replacement clutch. Occasional Cuckoo-host.
Nestlings sparse grey down; pale yellow inside the mouth, yellow gape-flanges. Remain in nest for 12 but usually 13–15 days.

Black Redstart* *Phoenicurus ochruros*
Pl. **72**
Site holes, crevices and ledges of buildings, many at a height of 2–6 m from the ground but up to

10 m in rock crevices of mountains. Sites include gardens, rafters, under eaves, disused Swallow nests and nestboxes. (Scattered breeding distribution in Britain, mainly in towns or on big modern buildings in rural areas.) *Nest* loosely made out of dry grass and rootlets, lined with plenty of hair or fur and sometimes feathers.

Eggs sometimes 4, generally 5–6; glossy surface, white or with faint shimmer of reddish-brown. Size 19·4 × 14·4 mm. Weight around 2 g. Incubation 13, occasionally 14, days. Two broods, mid-April–July. Replacement clutch. Occasional Cuckoo-host.

Nestlings sparse bluish-grey down, dark yellow inside mouth, pale yellow gape-flanges. Remain in nest for 13–16 days, 12–17 days have been recorded.

Wheatear* *Oenanthe oenanthe*
Pl. **70, 188**

Site in a hole at ground level or up to 70 cm, always protected from above. Holes may be in stone walls, rubbish dumps, piles of stones, banks of earth or in disused rabbit burrows.

Nest hole is stuffed with dry grass and rootlets, sometimes moss, and lined with animal hair and feathers.

Eggs 5–6, less commonly 7; uniform pale blue, sometimes almost white. Size 21·2 × 15·9 mm. Weight 2·0–3·0 g. Incubation 14 days. Usually single-brooded, April/May–June/July, sometimes two broods. Replacement clutch. Rare Cuckoo-host.

Nestlings whitish-grey down on head and back, yellow inside mouth, yellow gape-flanges. Remain in nest for 14–16 days.

Stonechat* *Saxicola torquata*
Pl. **79**

Site often at the foot of a bush, on or near the ground in a hollow hidden by tall grass; frequently on some kind of a slope, such as an embankment or hillside.

Nest made out of moss, dry grass, rootlets and dead leaves, lined with fine bents and animal hair, sometimes with feathers.

Eggs sometimes 4, usually 5–6; greenish-grey ground colour, finely speckled or densely marked reddish-brown. Size 18·9 × 14·4 mm. Weight 2·0 g. Incubation 14–15 days. Usually two broods, April–July, but a third and a fourth have been recorded. Occasional Cuckoo-host.

Nestlings sparse whitish-grey down; yellow inside mouth, yellow gape-flanges. Remain in nest for occasionally 10, usually 11–15 days.

Whinchat* *Saxicola rubetra*
Pl. **80**

Site similar to Stonechat, in a small hollow, hidden under tall grass.

Nest similar to Stonechat but lining of fine grass and hair is polished smooth.

Eggs 5–7, less frequently 4; deep greenish-blue ground colour, finely speckled reddish-brown, markings often zoned at blunt end. Size 19·2 × 14·8 mm. Weight around 2 g. Incubation

13, but sometimes 14, days. Usually single-brooded, May–June/July. Replacement clutch Occasional Cuckoo-host.

Nestlings sparse grey down, yellow inside mouth, with two dark spots on tongue and yellow gape-flanges. Remain in nest for about 12 days.

Blackbird* *Turdus merula*
Pl. **74**

Site frequently in bush or tree, mostly 1–3 m from the ground, and on ivy-clad walls or tree-stumps; in hedgerows, woods and gardens where it is often in a shrub growing against a wall. A number of unusual sites have been recorded and some nests are at ground level.

Nest small twigs, rootlets, moss and dry leaves form a bulky outer layer which is then made firm and smooth on the inside with damp earth; finally, bits of grass are often added as a soft inner lining.

Eggs 4–6; greenish-blue ground colour with variable markings; the latter are usually bold, such as reddish-brown spots or dark blotches and shell-marks. Size 28·6 × 21·0 mm. Weight 9 g. Incubation 13–14 days. Two to three broods, March–July.

Nestlings sparse dark grey down; yellow inside mouth, yellow gape-flanges. Remain in nest for 13–16 days.

Ring Ouzel* *Turdus torquatus*
Pl. **208**

Site frequently in bushes or small trees, close to the trunk, at a height of 2 m from the ground; also at ground level in clumps of heather or similar moorland vegetation. Other sites include stone walls and mineshafts. (Associated with uplands in Br. Is.)

Nest same type as Blackbird; made out of local stems or twigs and grass, sometimes decorated on the outside with lichen, solidified with layer of earth before lined with fine bents and fibres. Intermediate layer of earth sometimes absent.

Eggs occasionally 3, generally 4–5; greenish-blue ground colour with reddish markings, reminiscent of Blackbird. Size 30·4 × 21·5 mm. Weight 8 g. Incubation 14 days. One to two broods, April/May–June/July. Cuckoo-host occasionally.

Nestlings buff down; yellow inside mouth, paler gape-flanges. Remain in nest for 14–15 days.

Mistle Thrush* *Turdus viscivorus*
Pl. **207**

Site in bare fork of tall trees, usually close to trunk at a height of 1–10 m from the ground; also recorded in low bushes and on ledges of cliffs and buildings.

Nest bulky outer layer of twigs or stems, roots, moss and grass, strengthened with a variable amount of earth and lined with fine bents. Sometimes rags or bits of paper, lichen and feathers are also incorporated.

Eggs 3–5; ground colour usually greenish-blue sometimes pale reddish-brown, with irregular pattern of purplish-grey shell-marks and bolder blotches of reddish-brown. Size 31·2 × 22·3 mm. Weight 7 g. Incubation 13–14 days. Two broods, March–June. Replacement clutch.

Nestlings sparse pale buff down, bright yellow inside mouth, pale yellow gape-flanges. Remain in nest for 14–16 days.

Fieldfare* *Turdus pilaris*
Pl. **73**

Site colonies of varying size nest in trees growing in comparatively open stands, usually in woodland but also recorded in parks, etc. in built-up areas on the Continent. Tree species include birch, alder, oak, willow, larch and spruce. Height of nests varies between 3 m and about 10 m, often close to the trunk but also in forks of outer branches. Nests on the ground above tree limit. (Rare and local in northern areas of Br. Is.)

Nest similar to Blackbird.

Eggs 5–6, sometimes 7; greenish-blue ground colour with reddish markings, often difficult to distinguish from Blackbird. Size 28·8 × 20·9 mm. Weight 7 g. Incubation 13–14 days. One to two broods, late April–June. Replacement clutch.

Nestlings sparse buff down; bright yellow inside mouth, paler gape-flanges. Remain in nest for 14 days.

Song Thrush* *Turdus philomelos*
Pl. **75**

Site frequently in bush or tree up to 2 m from the ground but some-times higher when in built-up area (recorded at 6 m in a pear tree, by Hoeher). Sites are similar to Blackbird and include ivy-clad walls or tree-stumps, hedgerows, woods, parks and gardens. Nests are also recorded on the ground.

Nest outer layer of twigs, grass and moss is plastered inside with thick wall of mud mixed with dung and saliva. This results in a neat, hard lining which is some-what paler in colour than in other species and more like a cemented layer of mud.

Eggs 4–6; blue or greenish-blue ground colour, typically marked with a few black spots (some have dark brown and grey markings). Size 27·3 × 20·4 mm. Weight around 6·5 g. Incubation 12–13 days. Two broods, March/April–July.

Nestlings scanty yellowish-buff down, yellow inside mouth, paler gape-flanges. Remain in nest for 13–14, less often 15 days.

Redwing* *Turdus iliacus*
Pl. **206**

Site usually in bushes or trees, deciduous or conifer, at a height of 1 m but also at ground level. Favours open woodland and marshy ground where nests are often in rotting tree-stumps. Spreads into parks and gardens in built-up areas in Scandinavia. (Breeds locally in Scotland.)

Nest same type as Blackbird; made out of small twigs and stalks, moss and lichen, solidified with layer of earth and then lined with fine bents.

Eggs usually 5, occasionally 6–7;

greenish ground colour, finely marked with reddish-brown; look like small Blackbird's eggs. Size 25·8 × 19·2 mm. Weight around 6·5 g. Incubation 13 days. Usually single-brooded, late May–July, occasionally two broods.

Nestlings buff down; yellow inside mouth, paler gape-flanges. Remain in nest for 12–14 days.

Rock Thrush *Monticola saxatilis*
Pl. **204**
Site in a hole or crevice, usually on sunny slopes at high altitudes, in alpine meadows among vegetation or in rock crevices; also in stone walls and occasionally in ruined buildings at lower altitudes.

Nest neatly made out of grass, fibrous roots and moss.

Eggs sometimes 4, most commonly 5–6; uniform pale greenish-blue. Size 25·9 × 19·5 mm. Incubation 14–15 days. Probably single-brooded, May–June.

Nestlings bluish-grey down; dull yellow inside mouth, paler gape-flanges. Remain in nest for about 13–16 days.

WARBLERS   *Sylviidae*

The term 'warbler', used in a general sense, covers various types which are classified under separate genera *Sylvia, Hippolais, Locustella, Acrocephalus, Phylloscopus*; in addition, two *Regulus* species (Goldcrest, Firecrest) are sometimes included. The majority of warblers' nests are at a low height, in ground cover or above water (Reed Warbler). There are species which nest high up in trees (Goldcrest, Firecrest) or occasionally do so (Orphean Warbler). The shapes of nests also vary: a nearly round ball of moss, etc. (Goldcrest, Firecrest); domed or oval nests mainly of grass and leaves (*Phylloscopus*); deeper nests attached to stems of reeds, etc. (*Acrocephalus*); comparatively shallow, open bowl type (*Locustella*) and, often incorporating plant down (*Sylvia*). The majority of species have a pale ground colour and dark markings on the eggs. The average clutch-size for most species is 4–6, with 8–10 for Goldcrest and Firecrest. Twenty-one species breed in central Europe; twelve species breed regularly in Br. Is. (In addition, Dartford Warbler *Sylvia undata* breeds in parts of S. England but is not listed below.)

Goldcrest* *Regulus regulus*
Pl. **146**
Site usually very high, 10–12 m from the ground, in the upper branches of conifers (fir, spruce), suspended from the end of a branch, hidden by foliage. Other sites include ivy on tree-trunk and gorse-bush.

Nest nearly round, with a small entrance at the top, made out of moss, lichen and spiders' webs; this outer wall is about 4 cm thick, leaving an inner depression of 6 cm which is softly lined with hair, plant down and feathers.

Eggs 8–11; yellowish or white ground colour with a zone of fine reddish-brown markings at the blunt end. Size 13·6 × 10·3 mm. Weight 0·72 g. Incubation 16 days. Two broods, April–June/July.

Nestlings short grey down; pale orange inside mouth, lemon gape-flanges. Remain in nest for 18–20 days.

Firecrest* *Regulus ignicapillus*
Pl. **145**

Site similar to Goldcrest, suspended from tip of conifer branch (fir, spruce) often 10 m above the ground but also lower down. Other sites include ivy on tree and juniper bush; rarely in deciduous tree. (Irregular breeding in southern counties of England.)

Nest similar construction, slightly smaller than Goldcrest (inner depression 4 cm). Outer wall made out of moss, lichen and fibres (birch) matted with spiders' webs; inner lining of hair, plant down and feathers.

Eggs 7–12; similar to Goldcrest except for pinkish tinge in ground colour. Size 13·5 × 10·3 mm (the smallest egg of any European species). Weight 0·70 g. Incubation 14–15 days. Two broods, May–July. Replacement clutch.

Nestlings similar to Goldcrest. Remain in nest for 19–20, less often 18, days.

Chiffchaff* *Phylloscopus collybita*
Pl. **94**

Site just above the ground in low cover, on the edge of woodland or along hedgerow; often between brambles or grass growing up through branches and sometimes in very young trees.

Nest rounded or oval structure with a side entrance towards the top; eggs are visible through this hole (unlike Willow Warbler and Wood Warbler). Nest made out of grass, dead leaves and moss, lined with hair and feathers.

Eggs 5–6, more rarely 7; white ground colour faintly marked with purplish-grey and fine reddish-brown spots, often zoned at the blunt end. Size 15·5 × 12·0 mm. Weight 1·2–1·4 g. Incubation 13–14 days. Often two broods, April/May—June/July. Cuckoo-host occasionally.

Nestlings naked except for pale yellow down on head and back; lemon inside mouth and very pale gape-flanges. Remain in nest for about 13–16 days.

Willow Warbler* *Phylloscopus trochilus*
Pl. **95, 253**

Site on the ground, hidden by grass, usually in deciduous woodland or on rough ground with plenty of cover, but also in young conifer plantations.

Nest similar to Chiffchaff but looks more domed; eggs are not visible through the entrance-hole at the side which is round (not oval). Same nesting material as Chiffchaff.

Eggs sometimes 5, usually 6–7; yellowish-white ground colour, reddish spots tend to be more strongly marked than Chiffchaff. Size 15·3 × 12·4 mm. Weight 1·0–1·1 g. Incubation 13 days. Usually single-brooded, May–

June, but sometimes two broods. Replacement clutch. Cuckoo-host occasionally but nest often deserted after Cuckoo's egg has been laid in it.

Nestlings yellowish skin, sparse down on head and neck; orange-yellow inside mouth, yellow gape-flanges. Remain in nest for 18–19 days.

Bonelli's Warbler *Phylloscopus bonelli*
Pl. **155**

Site on the ground in pine forests or among scrub vegetation in scree above the tree-limit.

Nest oval structure, which looks like Wood Warbler's nest, with a small entrance-hole at the side towards the top; made out of dead leaves, moss and bents (no lining material).

Eggs 5–6, less frequently 7; whitish ground colour with reddish-brown spots (markings less clearly defined than Wood Warbler). Size 15·0 × 11·8 mm. Weight around 1·2 g. Incubation 13, or sometimes 14 days. Single brood, May–June. Replacement clutch.

Nestlings remain in nest for 12 days.

Wood Warbler* *Phylloscopus sibilatrix*
Pl. **96**

Site on the ground, hidden by grass or light cover, usually in deciduous woodland in a comparatively open site.

Nest same shape as Willow Warbler, domed appearance with entrance-hole at the side;

the eggs are barely visible through the hole which is oval, not round. Made out of grass and leaves, lined with fine bents and hair (no feathers).

Eggs 5–6, occasionally 7; white ground colour densely marked with reddish-brown spots and sometimes a few purplish-grey marks. Size 16·1 × 12·6 mm. Weight around 1·3 g. Incubation 13 days. Usually single-brooded, May–June, rarely two broods. Cuckoo-host occasionally.

Nestlings yellowish-pink skin, naked except for scanty grey down on head and neck; lemon inside mouth and very pale gape-flanges. Remain in nest for 11–12 days.

Icterine Warbler *Hippolais icterina*
Pl. **87**

Site 1–2 m from the ground, usually in a fork, sometimes in a tree but more often in leafy shrub or bush (lilac, elder) in gardens and hedgerows. (Suspected of breeding in southern England.)

Nest same type as Reed Warbler; deep cup, neatly and firmly woven, always decorated on the outside with bark fibres (birch). Grass and fibres are woven together and felted with small feathers, hair, down and spiders' webs; sometimes there is a neat inner lining of dry grass.

Eggs 3–6; dull pinkish ground colour, sparsely marked with black spots and smaller flecks. Size 18·5 × 13·4 mm. Weight around 1·5–1·9 g. Incubation 13 days. Usually single-brooded, late May–June, rarely two broods. Replacement clutch. Cuckoo-host occasionally.

Nestlings no down; pale orange inside mouth with two black spots, yellow gape-flanges. Remain in nest for 13–14 days.

Marsh Warbler* *Acrocephalus palustris*

Pl. **85** (nest with Cuckoo's egg)

Site in dense cover of rank vegetation near water (reeds, nettles, etc.) in a few localities in Br. Is. and also in cereal crops (wheat, rye) on the Continent. Nests are usually about 1 m from the ground, attached to several stems of the plant.

Nest same type as Reed Warbler, made out of grass and stalks, lined with finer grass and hair.

Eggs 4–5, more rarely 6; bluish-white ground colour with olive-brown blotches and grey flecks; ground colour under markings is sometimes greenish. Size 18·9 × 13·5 mm. Weight approx. 1·8 g. Incubation 12, occasionally 13 days. Single brood, late May–June. Cuckoo-host frequently.

Nestlings no down, pink skin; pale orange inside mouth with two black spots, yellowish-white gape-flanges. Remain in nest for about 12 days.

Reed Warbler* *Acrocephalus scirpaceus*

Pl. **84**

Site frequently in reeds standing in water but also in rank vegetation near water, including bushes and small trees, and occasionally some distance from water. Nests are usually about 1 m from the ground, attached to several stems of the plant.

Nest 6 cm long attached to 2–3 stems (occasionally 4); bits of dead plants (reeds, etc.) and fibres, also moss and grass tussocks, lined with animal hair and plant down.

Eggs 3–5; dingy white ground colour (also greenish or bluish tinge), blotched or marbled with olive-brown and grey; thickly marked all over or blotched mainly at the blunt end. Size 18·3 × 13·6 mm. Weight 1·7–1·9 g. Incubation 11–12 days. Usually single-brooded, late May–June, occasionally two broods. Replacement clutch. Cuckoo-host frequently.

Nestlings no down, dull pink skin; bright yellow inside mouth, pale yellow gape-flanges. Remain in nest for 11–13 days.

Great Reed Warbler
Acrocephalus arundinaceus

Pl. **83**

Site in strong growth of reeds near open water, less frequently in bushes or trees, attached to several stems at heights varying from 0·5–1·5 m.

Nest larger than Reed Warbler, about 12–20 cm long, attached to 5 stems; cylindrical structure made out of bits of dead plants (reeds, etc.), fibres and grass tussocks, lined with seeding heads and plant down.

Eggs 4–6; bluish-white or greenish ground colour, blotched and flecked with olive-brown and blackish-grey markings which may be concentrated at the blunt end. Size 22·6 × 16·3 mm. Weight 3·0–3·3 g. Incubation 14–15 days. Usually single-brooded, mid-May–June, occasionally a second brood (according to Noll-Tobler). Cuckoo-host frequently.

Nestlings no down, yellow inside mouth with two black spots, lemon gape-flanges. Remain in nest for 12 days.

Sedge Warbler* *Acrocephalus schoenobaenus*
Pl. **86**

Site reedbeds and dense vegetation near water, including thickets of alder and willow; less frequently on dry ground in tangled undergrowth and also in growing crops. Nest is placed low above the ground, lodged in dense cover and not attached to several stems (see Reed Warbler).

Nest foundation layer of stems, moss and grass, lined with plant down and feathers.

Eggs 4–6; whitish ground colour but so densely marked that the eggs look almost uniform yellowish-grey or greyish-brown; sometimes there are black hair-lines. (Distinct resemblance to Yellow Wagtail eggs.) Size 17·7 × 13·1 mm. Weight around 1·5 g. Incubation 12–13 days. Usually single-brooded, May–June, but possibility of a second brood. Cuckoo-host frequently.

Nestlings no down, dark yellow inside mouth with two black spots, pale yellow gape-flanges. Remain in nest for 10–15, sometimes 16 days.

Aquatic Warbler *Acrocephalus paludicola*
Pl. **157**

Site tussocks of sedge, lodged between overhanging stems up to a height of about 1 m, on boggy ground of comparatively open marshes.

Nest smaller than Sedge Warbler but same type; built on loose foundation of dead bits of plants, grass and moss added, lining of seeding heads of grass and feathers, sometimes plant down also.

Eggs 5, less often 6; whitish ground colour but so densely marked that the eggs look almost uniform yellowish-grey or greyish-brown (difficult to distinguish from Sedge Warbler). Size 17·4 × 13·2 mm. Weight 1·3 × 1·8 g. Incubation 12–13 days. Possibly single-brooded, mid-May–June. Cuckoo-host rarely.

Nestlings remain in nest for about 14 days.

Savi's Warbler* *Locustella luscinioides*
Pl. **189**

Site extensive reedbeds and swamps with alder and willow bushes; low down among tangled remains of previous year's growth of reed, sedge, etc. (A few pairs in Suffolk and Kent.)

Nest comparatively bulky, made out of dead leaves of sedge, lined with finer leaves and grasses.

Eggs sometimes 3, generally 4–5; whitish ground colour, densely marked with greyish-brown or brown spots; sometimes more heavily marked at the blunt end.

Size 19·7 × 14·5 mm. Incubation approx. 12 days. Two
broods, May–July.
Nestlings remain in nest for 10–13
days.

River Warbler *Locustella fluviatilis*
Pl. **81, 191**

Site damp places with tangled
undergrowth, hidden in low
cover either on the ground or
just above it. Sites include banks
near water, forest clearings,
underwoods and more open
ground, provided there are
patches of bramble or rank
vegetation.
Nest same type as Grasshopper
Warbler, made out of dead
leaves, stalks and dry grasses,
lined with finer grass and sometimes with moss.
Eggs 4–5; whitish or pinkish-
white ground colour, dotted with
small brownish-grey spots. Size
20·0 × 15·1 mm. Incubation
around 12–13 days. Single brood,
late May—June/July.
Nestlings remain in nest for about
12 days.

Grasshopper Warbler*
Locustella naevia
Pl. **82, 190, 252**

Site hidden in low cover on damp
or dry ground, sheltered by
brambles, nettles or bushy undergrowth. Sites include marshes
and damp meadows, forest clearings or young plantations, heaths
and moors.
Nest made out of dry stems and
leaves, sometimes with moss, and
a smooth lining of finer bents.

Eggs 5–6, occasionally 7; pinkish
ground colour densely spotted
with small reddish-brown flecks.
Size 18·1 × 13·8 mm. Weight
1·7 g. Incubation 13–15 days.
Generally single-brooded, May–
July, but two broods in some
localities. Replacement clutch.
Nestlings greyish down on head
and back; bright yellow inside
mouth, with three black spots,
pale yellow gape-flanges. Remain
in nest for 10–12 days.

Lesser Whitethroat* *Sylvia curruca*
Pl. **93**

Site thorny thickets of whitethorn
and blackthorn in overgrown
hedgerows or on commons; also
in gooseberry bushes, ornamental
shrubs (box) and young spruce
trees. Nests are mostly 50 cm–1 m
above the ground, hidden by
foliage.
Nest smaller and shallower than
Whitethroat, but of similar construction; loosely made out of
fine rootlets, dead stems of plants,
grass and spiders' webs.
Eggs generally 5–6, sometimes 4;
whitish or creamy ground colour
marked with grey and brown
spots; there may also be black
hair-lines. Size 16·5 × 12·6 mm.
Weight around 1·7 g. Incubation
10–11, sometimes 12, days.
Usually single-brooded, May–
June, sometimes two broods. Replacement clutch. Cuckoo-host
rarely.
Nestlings no down; yellow inside
mouth with two dark spots,
yellow gape-flanges. Remain in
nest for 11 days.

Whitethroat* *Sylvia communis*
Pl. **90, 183**

Site thorny scrub and small bramble bushes (particularly with long grass growing up through them), tangled undergrowth of hedgerows and rough verges of woodland; usually less than 50 cm from the ground and often only a few cm up, hidden by stinging nettles or grass.

Nest loosely made out of small dry stems, grass and fine rootlets, entwined with plant down and spiders' webs, smoothly lined with hair (often horsehair); deeper cup than Lesser Whitethroat.

Eggs 4–5, less commonly 6; ground colour varies from greenish-grey or olive-brown to russet-yellow or drab yellow; markings are dark grey or brownish spots and blotches, often more dense at the blunt end. Size 18·1 × 13·8 mm. Weight around 2 g. Incubation 11–13 days. Two broods, early May–July.

Nestlings no down, pink skin; pinkish-yellow inside mouth with two blackish spots, yellow gape-flanges. Remain in nest for 10–12 days.

Barred Warbler *Sylvia nisoria*
Pl. **88**

Site thorn bushes (blackthorn, whitethorn, bramble, briar), often with hops or other climbing plants rambling over them, along hedgerows, in woodland clearings and on banks of streams; also in other bushes (e.g. alder) in parks, gardens and cemeteries. Nests are mostly 50–80 cm from the

ground, rarely higher than 1 m.

Nest bulky but compactly built out of small stems and bents, with a smooth lining of root fibres and animal hair.

Eggs 4–6; greenish-white or greyish-white ground colour with grey flecks and olive-brown blotches. Size 21·1 × 14.4 mm. Weight 2·5 g. Incubation 14–15 days. Single brood, May–June. Cuckoo-host frequently.

Nestlings remain in nest for 11–13 days.

Garden Warbler* *Sylvia borin*
Pl. **89, 184**

Site often on patches of brambles and nettles, in fruit bushes and shrubs (gooseberry and elder), also in young conifer plantations and occasionally in epicormic growth on tree-trunks. Nests are mostly between 40 cm and 120 cm from the ground.

Nest comparatively open bowl made out of grass and bents with a little moss, lined with finer grass and hair.

Eggs, 4–5, less usually 6; ground colour varies from whitish or greenish-white to yellowish, markings give marbled effect in various shades of brown (difficult to distinguish from Blackcap). Size 20·1 × 14·8 mm. Weight 2·4–2·6 g. Incubation 12 days. Usually single-brooded, May–June/July, occasionally two broods. Replacement clutch. Cuckoo-host frequently.

Nestlings no down; bright red inside mouth, yellowish gape-flanges. Remain in nest for 10–12 days.

Orphean Warbler *Sylvia hortensis*

Pl. **185**

Site on bushes or lower branches of trees in the Mediterranean area. Sites include woodland with plenty of undergrowth, olive trees in orchards and fruit bushes in gardens. Some nests are at a considerable height from the ground (unlike other *Sylvia* species).

Nest neatly woven out of grass, bents, rootlets and fibres.

Eggs 4–5; greenish-white ground colour with dark brown to blackish spots. Size 19·0 × 14·4 mm. Incubation 12 days. Single brood, May.

Nestlings remain in nest for 11–15 days.

Blackcap* *Sylvia atricapilla*

Pl. **91, 92**

Site much the same habitat as Garden Warbler but, on average, nests of Blackcap tend to be higher. Sites include woodland, parks, gardens and cemeteries, frequently in brambles or thorn bushes, also in young conifer plantations and in epicormic growth on beech and elm trees.

Nest neater structure than Garden Warbler; nesting material includes grass, bents, fibrous roots, plant down, spiders' webs and hair.

Eggs 4–6; ground colour varies from pale brown to greenish-white or stone grey, marked with dark brown and grey spots; some markings are so dark that the spots look as if they had been burned on with a branding iron (see Pl. 91). Size 19·6 × 14·7 mm. Weight 1·8–2·1 g. Incubation 14–15 days, according to Makatsch. Two broods, early May–June/July. Replacement clutch. Cuckoo-host occasionally.

Nestlings no down; pinkish-yellow inside mouth. Remain in nest for 10–13 days.

FLYCATCHERS
Muscicapidae

Flycatchers occupy holes or niches and show little artistry in building their nests.

Key to eggs: greenish with reddish blotches (Spotted Flycatcher); yellowish-white with lots of reddish-brown spots (Red-breasted Flycatcher); uniform pale blue (Pied Flycatcher, Collared Flycatcher). Clutch-size mostly 5–6 eggs. One brood per year, except for Spotted Flycatcher which sometimes has two broods. Four species breed in central Europe; two species breed in Br. Is.

Spotted Flycatcher* *Muscicapa striata*

Pl. **115**

Site niches in leafy cover against walls, among ivy or behind loose bark on tree-trunk, and some-times in comparatively open site of a fork in a tree; also recorded on rafters, in small cavities and open-type nestboxes. Many nests are found at heights between 1·50 m and 3 m from the ground.

Nest loosely arranged material; rootlets, wool fibres, grass and hair, neatly lined with plant down and hair.

Eggs 4–5, sometimes 6; greenish ground colour with lots of reddish spots and isolated shell-marks of greyish-purple. Size 18·4 × 13·6 mm. Weight around 2 g. Incubation 12–13 days. Usually single-brooded, May–June, but second brood not uncommon. Cuckoo-host occasionally.

Nestlings scanty grey down; dark yellow inside mouth with lemon yellow triangular patch on tongue, pale yellow gape-flanges. Remain in nest for 11–14 days.

Pied Flycatcher* *Ficedula hypoleuca*
Pl. **116**

Site holes in rotting trees, including Lesser Spotted Woodpecker holes, and in nestboxes (hole-type). In Br. Is. mainly confined to old deciduous trees in hilly country of the north and west.

Nest loosely arranged material; dry grass, dead leaves, rootlets and fibres, lined with finer material, such as hair and grasses.

Eggs 5–6, less often 7; uniform pale blue. Size 17·6 × 12·7 mm. Weight 1·5 g. Incubation 13, sometimes 14–15, days. Single brood, May–June. Replacement clutch.

Nestlings scanty grey down on head and back, dark yellow inside mouth, pale yellow gape-flanges. Remain in nest for 14–16 days.

Collared Flycatcher *Ficedula albicollis*
Pl. **117**

Site holes in trees, often at considerable height but also lower down in tree-stumps; hole is narrower at entrance than for next species. Also uses hole-type nestboxes.

Nest similar to Pied Flycatcher.

Eggs 5–6, less usually 7; uniform pale blue. Size 17·8 × 12·1 mm. Weight around 1·5 g. Incubation period and number of broods similar to Pied Flycatcher.

Nestlings remain in nest for 14–16 days.

Red-breasted Flycatcher
Ficedula parva
Pl. **158**

Site height of hole or niche varies from 2–10 m above the ground; entrance to hole is wider than for previous species. High up in beech, lime and oak; holes and crevices in rotting wood, and occasionally in more open site of a fork, close to the trunk of a beech tree. This species also uses nestboxes.

Nest loosely arranged material; fine grass and moss, lined with hair.

Eggs 5–6, occasionally 7, yellowish-white ground colour, finely speckled with reddish spots, like a small version of Robin's egg. Size 16·6 × 12·6 mm. Weight approx. 1·5–1·7 g. Incubation 12 days. Single brood, late May–early June. Replacement clutch.

Nestlings remain in nest for 13 days.

ACCENTORS *Prunellidae*

There are two breeding species in central Europe, one of which also breeds in Br. Is. Nests are always well-hidden, either at ground level or just above, neatly made out of moss and fine twigs or stems. Dunnock nests in hedges or bushes; Alpine Accentor nests in holes or crevices of rocky ground in mountains of central Europe. There are 4–5 eggs per clutch, deep blue-green and unmarked. Dunnock has two broods per year; Alpine Accentor is single-brooded.

Dunnock* *Prunella modularis*
Pl. **112**

Site in bushes, hedges, bramble patches and similar undergrowth, also in young trees; usually up to a height of 1 m from the ground and always well-hidden.

Nest neat structure of moss and fine twigs, lined with bents and hair. Some nests are lined with feathers or the red spore-capsules of moss.

Eggs 4–5, less commonly 6; uniform deep blue-green. Size 19·9 × 14·7 mm. Weight 2·0 g. Incubation 12–14 days. Two broods, sometimes three, March–August. Cuckoo-host frequently.

Nestlings scanty long black down, orange inside mouth, pinkish gape-flanges. Remain in nest for 11–14 days.

Alpine Accentor *Prunella collaris*
Pl. **111**

Site in mountains, between rocks on the ground or in rock crevices and sometimes in bushy scrub.

Nest similar to Dunnock, neatly made out of bents, moss and rootlets, lined with moss, hair and sometimes with feathers.

Eggs 4–5, sometimes 6; uniform deep blue-green. Size 23·2 × 16·6 mm. Weight 3·3 g. Incubation about 14 days. Normally single-brooded, late May–July, second brood rare.

Nestlings remain in nest for 11–16 days.

PIPITS AND WAGTAILS *Motacillidae*

Nests are built in small hollows on the ground, protected by tufts of vegetation or clods of earth, and in niches or crevices which are often on man-made sites (walls, bridges, etc.). In general, Pipits nest on the ground and Wagtails in niches above the ground; Blue-headed and Yellow Wagtails are the exception, favouring hollows on the ground. Nesting material of Pipits usually consists of grass and rootlets. Wagtails often incorporate moss in their nests, and all species use hair as lining material. Eggs are very variable: the ground colour is whitish or drab, all having markings, many of which are so dense that the ground colour may be virtually obliterated. Clutch-size mostly 4–6 eggs. One to two broods per year. Ten species breed in central Europe; two of these (Tawny and Water Pipits) do not breed in Br. Is.

174

Tawny Pipit *Anthus campestris*
Pl. **173, 174**
Site small depression in the ground, often among young cereal crops but also on dry waste ground. Nests are hidden by tufts of vegetation or earth tussocks.
Nest foundation of rootlets and grass, with a layer of moss and grass, lined with hair (often horsehair) and fine bents.
Eggs 4–5, sometimes 6; whitish ground colour with purplish-grey shell-marks and brown mottling; markings are often more clearly defined than in other Pipits and less dense than Meadow Pipit but overall mottling occurs (see Pl. 174). Size 21·9 × 15·7 mm. Incubation 13–14 days. Usually single-brooded, June, occasionally two broods. Cuckoo-host occasionally.
Nestlings remain in nest for about 13 days.

Water Pipit *Anthus spinoletta spinoletta*
Pl. **175**
Site in mountain areas of central Europe; in short grass of alpine meadows, among low scrub or between stones and boulders on barren ground. Nests are often near mountain streams, hidden by stones or overhanging grass.
Nest more bulky than Tree Pipit or Meadow Pipit, made out of grass and moss, lined with fine bents and sometimes hair.
Eggs 4–6; dull white ground colour, closely mottled with fine brown and grey spots. Size 21·3 × 15·5 mm. Weight 2·7 g. Incu-

bation approx. 13–14 days. Two broods, mid-May–June.
Nestlings remain in nest for about 14 days.

Rock Pipit* *Anthus spinoletta petrosus*
Pl. **176**
Site rocky coasts, on or near the shore, in crevices between rocks or hidden by vegetation, occasionally on cliff-tops.
Nest comparatively well-built with a thick layer of grassy rootlets and bits of wrack, lined with fine bents and sometimes hair.
Eggs 4–5, less commonly 6; greyish-white ground colour, densely covered with fine brown and grey spots. Size 21·3 × 15·9 mm. Weight 2·8 g. Incubation 15 days (according to Heinroth). Two broods, April–June/July.
Nestlings long greyish-brown down, reddish inside mouth, pale yellow gape-flanges. Remain in nest for 14–15, occasionally 16 days.

Meadow Pipit* *Anthus pratensis*
Pl. **136, 177, 178**
Site rough grass on moors, damp pastures, heaths and dunes. Nests are hidden under grass tufts and very difficult to find.
Nest comparatively loosely built, chiefly of grass and bents, nearly always lined with hair.
Eggs 4–6; greyish-white or brownish-yellow ground colour which is frequently obliterated by dark brown mottling (Pl. 136); occasionally there are black hairlines at the blunt end. Eggs of

this species are very variable but usually look somewhat smaller and more slender than other Pipits (Tawny, Water and Tree). Size 19·8 × 14·6 mm. Weight 2 g. Incubation 13–14 days. Two broods, April–June/July. Replacement clutch. Cuckoo-host frequently.

Nestlings scanty pale grey down, pink skin; bright orange-red inside mouth, dark yellow gape-flanges. Remain in nest for 12–15 days.

Tree Pipit* *Anthus trivialis*
Pl. **135, 179, 180, 255**

Site among rough grass, heather and bracken, on ground with bushes and trees; also in tall grass on verges and in woodland clearings. Nests are hidden under tussocks or in low vegetation.

Nest comparatively loosely built; made of grass, moss and bents, lined with finer grass and hair, occasionally also with plant down.

Eggs sometimes 4, generally 5–6; very variable in colour and markings, greyish-white, pinkish-grey or pale green ground colour, with large dark blotches, irregular spots and scrawls, sometimes with black 'scorch-marks' (see illustrations). Size 20·7 × 15·5 mm. Weight 2·3 g. Incubation 13–14 days. Usually single-brooded, early May—June/July. Cuckoo-host rarely.

Nestlings thick dark grey down, pink skin; orange inside mouth, with yellow spot, pale yellow gape-flanges. Remain in nest for 12 days.

Blue-headed Wagtail*
Motacilla flava flava
Pl. **137**

Site damp meadows and arable fields in the vicinity of water, often on grass verges or banks, including railway embankments. Nests are on the ground in natural hollows, under grass tussock or beside a clod of earth. *Nest* made out of bents, rootlets and other plant material, lined with hair and fine bents.

Eggs 5–6; yellowish-white ground colour virtually obliterated by greyish-brown mottling, markings may include black hairlines. Size 18·7 × 13·9 mm. Weight 1·8 g. Incubation 13–14 days. Usually single-brooded, mid-April–June, but a second brood in July is a possibility. Cuckoo-host frequently.

Nestlings pale greyish-yellow down; orange inside mouth, yellow gape-flanges. Remain in nest for about 13 days.

Yellow Wagtail* *Motacilla flava flavissima*
Pl. **138**

Site similar to Blue-headed Wagtail, on the ground in a natural hollow, protected by herbage or clod of earth.

Nest made out of bents and rootlets, lined with hair.

Eggs sometimes 4, generally 5–6; similar to Blue-headed Wagtail. Size 19·1 × 14·3 mm. Weight around 1·9 g. Incubation 13–14 days. Usually single-brooded, mid-April–June, sometimes two broods July. Cuckoo-host occasionally.

Nestlings pale greyish-yellow down; orange inside mouth, pale yellow gape-flanges. Remain in nest for 12 days.

Grey Wagtail* *Motacilla cinerea*
Pl. **139**

Site usually in a cavity or niche close to water, seldom in the open. Sites include holes in walls and banks, niches or ledges under bridges, between tree-roots on river banks or by fast-running hill streams.

Nest material includes grasses, leaves, moss, rootlets, lined with hair and occasionally feathers.

Eggs sometimes 4, usually 5–6, rarely 7; yellowish ground colour, mottled greyish-brown (usually reminiscent of Yellow Wagtail but individual clutches vary). Size 19·0 × 14·5 mm. Weight 1·9 g. Incubation 12–14 days. Two broods, April–July. Cuckoo-host occasionally.

Nestlings yellow down; orange inside mouth, chrome-yellow gape-flanges. Remain in nest for 12–13 days.

White Wagtail* *Motacilla alba alba*
Pl. **140**

Site cavities and niches of various kinds, often 1–3 m from the ground; in walls, earth banks, holes in pollard willows, under tree-roots, in ivy, stacks of wood, inside open sheds and so on. (Interbreeds with next species.)

Nest simply constructed out of rootlets, bents, dry leaves, moss and fibres, lined with hair and feathers.

Eggs 5–6, sometimes 4 or 7; whitish ground colour, spotted and flecked all over with grey. Size 20·4 × 15·1 mm. Weight 2·2 g. Incubation 12–14 days. Two broods, mid-April–July, sometimes a third brood. Replacement clutch. Cuckoo-host frequently.

Nestlings whitish-grey down, pink skin; orange inside mouth with red triangular patch, pale yellow gape-flanges. Remain in nest for 14–15 days.

Pied Wagtail* *Motacilla alba yarrellii*
Pl. **192**

Site similar to White Wagtail.
Nest similar to White Wagtail.
Eggs 5–6; similar to White Wagtail in colour, markings, size, weight and incubation period. Normally two broods, April–July, but occasionally a third. Cuckoo-host frequently.
Nestlings similar to White Wagtail.

WAXWINGS
Bombycillidae

One species breeds in northern Europe (Lapland) in conifer forests on swampy ground. The nest is made out of twigs, lichen and moss, with a soft lining of hair, and built in a tree (usually in pine or spruce, occasionally in deciduous birch). There are 4–5 eggs per clutch, bluish-grey with a few black and grey markings, and one brood per year.

Waxwing *Bombycilla garrulus*
Pl. **203**
Site usually in pine or spruce tree, occasionally birch, in forests near swamps (Lapland). Nests are mostly 4–5 m from the ground. *Nest* made out of fine twigs, moss and lichen, lined with grass and reindeer hair.

Eggs 4–5, sometimes 6; bluish-grey ground colour, sparsely marked with grey and black spots and shell-marks. Size 24·0 × 17·3 mm. Weight 4·3 g. Incubation 13–14 days. Single brood, mid-June.
Nestlings remain in nest for 14–16(?) days.

SHRIKES *Laniidae*

Nests are in trees or thorn bushes, many at a height of about 2 m from the ground but higher (approx. 7 m) for Woodchat Shrike and Lesser Grey Shrike. Nesting material includes stalks, bents, roots, moss and feathers. Eggs are variable in ground colour (mostly greenish, yellowish or whitish), markings are also variable but are characteristically zoned at the blunt end. Shrikes are single-brooded; clutch-size mostly 5–7 eggs. Four species breed in central Europe; only Red-backed Shrike breeds in Br. Is.

Red-backed Shrike* *Lanius collurio*
Pl. **107, 196, 197**
Site thorny thickets of briars, brambles, whitethorn, blackthorn and other bushes (elder), overgrown with rampant climbers (hop, etc.); occasionally in young spruce or fruit trees. Height of nest varies but most are 50 cm–2 m from the ground. (Now confined to S.E. England.)
Nest made out of bents and stalks, mixed with moss and root fibres, lined with fine bents and hair. (Individual nests made only of stalks or moss are also found.)
Eggs 4–6, less frequently 7; characteristic zone of dark markings (grey and reddish-brown) on very variable ground colour (greenish, pinkish, yellowish). Size 22·9 × 17·1 mm. Weight 3·5 g. Incubation 14–15, occa-

sionally 16 days. Usually single-brooded, May–June/July. Replacement clutch. Cuckoo-host frequently.
Nestlings no down; dark yellow inside mouth, pale yellow gape-flanges. Remain in nest for about 15 days.

Woodchat Shrike *Lanius senator*
Pl. **109**
Site nearly always in trees, occasionally in bushes, at varying heights (several metres up); associated with dry, open country, often in orchards and trees planted in comparatively open situation.
Nest similar to Lesser Grey Shrike, sometimes with feathers included in lining.
Eggs 5–6, less often 7; greenish or brownish-yellow ground colour with characteristic zone of mark-

ings (greyish-brown and pale grey); very variable and some clutches are difficult to distinguish from Lesser Grey Shrike. Size 22·8 × 16·9 mm. Weight 3·4 g. Incubation 14–15 days. Single brood, May.
Nestlings remain in nest for 14–16 days.

Great Grey Shrike *Lanius excubitor*
Pl. **106**
Site bushes or trees at varying heights, mostly from 2–5 m from the ground; high up in conifer plantations, also in young birch trees and whitethorn thickets, occasionally in conifer or deciduous species growing on its own at the edge of a copse.
Nest Thrush-size, solidly built out of twigs and grass with a great many feathers, lined with softer feathers.
Eggs 5–6, less often 7; greyish-white ground colour with greyish brown blotches and pale grey shell-marks, markings more concentrated at the blunt end (reminiscent of Magpie eggs but

smaller). Size 26·3 × 19·3 mm. Weight 5·5 g. Incubation 15, sometimes 16–17 days. Single brood, mid-April–May. Replacement clutch. Cuckoo-host rarely.
Nestlings remain in nest for about 19 days.

Lesser Grey Shrike *Lanius minor*
Pl. **108**
Site high up in deciduous trees and in tall bushy thickets, mostly from 4 to 8 m from the ground. Nests may be close to the trunk or in outer branches of fruit trees, poplars and similar species.
Nest made out of small stems, bents and rootlets, often mixed with lots of plant bits such as thyme or mint; lined with fine fibrous material and hair, sometimes also with feathers.
Eggs 5–6, less often 7; pale green ground colour with pale grey and olive-brown blotches, markings often zoned at blunt end. Size 25·1 × 18·2 mm. Incubation 15 days. Single brood, May–June.
Nestlings remain in nest for about 16 days.

STARLINGS

Sturnidae

One species breeds in central Europe and Br. Is. Starlings nest in a great variety of holes, normally in colonies but also singly. Nesting material consists largely of straw and grass; fibres, feathers and other material may also be incorporated. There are usually 5–6 eggs, which are pale blue and unmarked, and one to two broods per year.

Starling* *Sturnus vulgaris*
Pl. **69**
Site holes in trees, including Woodpecker-holes, thatch on roofs, niches and crevices in walls, buildings, cliffs and so on.

Nestboxes are freely occupied, entrance-hole 4 cm wide.
Nest layer of straw and grass with bents and fibrous material, carelessly shaped into a cup which is lined with finer bents and

feathers; sometimes decorated with fresh blossom.

Eggs 5–6, sometimes 7; glossy surface, pale blue, unmarked. Size 29·6 × 21·1 mm. Weight 7·1 g. Incubation 14, occasionally 15 days. Single brood, April–May, sometimes two broods in various areas.

Nestlings naked except for a little grey down on head and back; bright yellow inside mouth, pale yellow gape-flange. Remain in nest for 21 days.

FINCHES   *Fringillidae*

The term 'Finch' covers a number of seed-eating species which build deep cups out of small twigs, rootlets, grass and moss (some are decorated with cobwebs). Nests are built in hedges, bushes and trees, singly or in small colonies (Redpolls, Twite, Brambling). Eggs are mostly bluish-white or greyish-green, with a zone of markings at the blunt end; those of Chaffinch and Brambling are very variable in colour and markings (the latter include brownish-black scrawls which look as though they were made with a branding iron). There are mostly two broods per year and 4–6 eggs per clutch. Thirteen species breed in central Europe; eleven of these breed regularly in Br. Is.

Hawfinch* *Coccothraustes coccothraustes*
Pl. **97, 98**

Site in various deciduous trees, often between 2·5m and 5 m from the ground, close to the trunk on a horizontal branch; sometimes higher up in outer branches of canopy.

Nest foundation of dry twigs, with a shallow cup of rootlets and hair.

Eggs sometimes 4, generally 5–6; usually greyish-green ground colour, sometimes pale blue or brownish-grey (see Plates 97 and 98), marked with a variety of distinctive spots and scrawls in grey, dark brown or black. Size 24·5 × 17·5 mm. Weight 3·2–3·5 g. Incubation 14 days. Single brood, April/May–June/July.

Nestlings covered with white down; brightly coloured gape (red, blue and orange), pink tongue edged with purple, yellow gape-flanges. Remain in nest for about 14 days.

Greenfinch* *Carduelis chloris*
Pl. **104**

Site frequently in bushes and hedges, sometimes in trees and among ivy, generally at a height of 1·5–3 m from the ground.

Nest fine roots and dry grass, interwoven with plenty of moss, sometimes a comparatively substantial structure on foundation of twigs, lined with plant down and animal hair.

Eggs 5, less often 6; bluish-white or drab white ground colour; amount of marking varies, often reddish-brown spots and purplish-grey shell-marks are zoned at the blunt end. Size 20·2 × 14·5 mm. Weight around 2 g.

Incubation 13–14 days. Two broods, April–July.

Nestlings long pale grey down; bright red inside mouth, yellow gape-flanges. Remain in nest for 13–14 days.

Linnet* *Acanthis cannabina*
Pl. **105**

Site low down in bushes or thickets, such as whitethorn and gorse, also in young plantations of conifer and deciduous species, among ivy and occasionally in heather or rough grass. Nests are mostly 0·5–2 m from the ground, often in small colonies.

Nest small twigs and rootlets, mixed with grass, moss and fibrous material; lined with plant down, animal hair and sometimes feathers.

Eggs sometimes 4, generally 5–6; bluish-white ground colour, usually with reddish-brown spots and streaks, occasionally unmarked. Size 17·7 × 13·3 mm. Weight 2 g. Incubation 12–14 days. Two broods, occasionally three, April–August. Cuckoo-host occasionally.

Nestlings long yellowish-grey down, pinkish-blue inside mouth, yellow gape-flanges. Remain in nest for 11–12 days.

Twite* *Acanthis flavirostris*
Pl. **159**

Site on or near the ground in low cover (heather, gorse) or between large stones, also in stone walls. Mainly found on moors or rough ground in northern areas. Nests are often in small colonies.

Nest similar to Linnet, made out of small twigs, rootlets, grass and moss, lined with animal fur and hair, sometimes feathers.

Eggs, 5–6, sometimes 7; bluish-white ground colour with reddish-brown spots and streaks, markings zoned at the blunt end; eggs look like Linnet except for bolder markings. Size 17·2 × 12·9 mm. Weight 1·5 g. Incubation 12–13 days. One or two broods, May–June or later.

Nestlings pale grey down; purplish inside mouth, whitish gape-flanges. Remain in nest for 15 days.

Redpoll (Mealy) *Carduelis flammea flammea*
Pl. **99**

Site in scrub growth or close to tree-trunk (birch, willow, alder) in northern latitudes. Nests are from 0·5–2 m above the ground, frequently in small colonies.

Nest solidly built of small twigs, bents and moss, lined with plant down and feathers; outer wall decorated with bark fibres, making it difficult to spot against the background.

Eggs occasionally 4, usually 5–6; blue ground colour, marked with reddish-brown spots or blotches, zoned at the blunt end. Size 16·9 × 12·6 mm. Weight 1·2–1·4 g. Incubation 10–11 days. One to two broods, May–June.

Nestlings red inside mouth; remain in nest for about 12 days.

Lesser Redpoll* *Carduelis flammea cabaret*
Pl. **193**

Site bushes, hedges and trees, often in conifer plantations. Nests are 2–3 m from the ground, frequently in small colonies.

Nest same as previous species.

Eggs similar colour and markings to Redpoll. Size 16·2 × 12·4 mm. Weight 1·3 g. Incubation in Alps 12–13, sometimes 14 days, generally single-brooded, mid-May–June; incubation in Br. Is. 10–11 days, one to two broods, April/May–June/July.

Nestlings grey down; red inside mouth, whitish gape-flanges. Remain in nest for about 12–13 days.

Siskin* *Carduelis spinus*
Pl. **162**

Site high up in outer branches of conifers, often in spruce but also in pine and larch. Nests are approximately 18–25 m from the ground.

Nest small but deep cup, neatly woven out of fine twigs, bents, moss, lichen, bark fibres and spiders' webs; lined with plant down, animal hair and feathers.

Eggs 4–5, occasionally 6; bluish-white ground colour with a zone of pale red and dark brown spots at the blunt end (similar to Goldfinch). Size 16·4 × 12·3 mm. Weight approx 1 g. Incubation 11–12 days. Two broods, April–June/July.

Nestlings scanty pale grey down; red inside mouth, yellow gape-flanges. Remain in nest for 12–13, less often 14 days.

Goldfinch* *Carduelis carduelis*
Pl. **101, 160**

Site usually in outer branches of trees, often in orchards, less fre-quently in bushes and hedges. Nests are difficult to see, hidden by foliage towards the end of a branch, mostly from 5–8 m above the ground.

Nest small and neat, made out of fine twigs, rootlets, bark fibres, moss and lichen, interwoven with spiders' webs and lined with plenty of plant down (often thistle).

Eggs usually 5–6, occasionally 4; thin-shelled, bluish-white ground colour, marked with grey shell-marks and reddish-brown spots. Size 17·0 × 12·8 mm. Weight 1·4 g. Incubation 12–13 days. Two broods, May–July.

Nestlings dark grey down; purplish and red inside mouth, creamy-white gape-flanges. Remain in nest for 13–14, sometimes 15 days.

Serin* *Serinus serinus*
Pl. **100, 156**

Site in bushes, shrubs and trees (elder, lilac, maple, vine, chestnut, spruce, pine). Nests are mostly 2–4 m from the ground, often on side branches, either close to the trunk or towards the outer edges. (Breeds occasionally in southern England.)

Nest made out of plant stems, bark fibres, rootlets and moss, lined with plant down, animal hair and feathers.

Eggs 4–5; bluish-white ground colour, marked with reddish and dark brown or black spots and streaks, zoned at the blunt end. Size 16·1 × 11·8 mm. Weight 1·2 g. Incubation 13 days. Two broods, April–July.

Nestlings pale grey down; dark red inside mouth, yellow gape-flanges. Remain in nest for 14 days.

Citril Finch *Serinus citrinella*
(Not illustrated)

Site in conifers (spruce), similar to Siskin but not quite as high up.
Nest made out of grass, lichen, moss and rootlets, often inter-woven with spiders' webs, and lined with plant down, animal hair and feathers.
Eggs 4–5; pale bluish ground colour, marked with reddish and dark brown spots (similar to Goldfinch). Size 16·5 × 12·6 mm. Incubation about 14 days. Probably two broods, late April–June.
Nestlings remain in nest for about 16 days.

Bullfinch* *Pyrrhula pyrrhula*
Pl. **195**

Site favours bushy growth of ever-greens, generally 1–2 m from the ground; bushes and trees (often yew, spruce, fir, juniper), and among rampant climbers (ivy, hop).
Nest light but firm foundation of dry twigs with a shallow cup of rootlets, similar to Hawfinch.
Eggs 4–5, sometimes 6; pale blue ground colour, sparsely marked with reddish-brown or black spots and grey streaks, zoned at the blunt end. Size 20·2 × 15·1 mm. Weight 2·1 g. Incubation 13 days. Two broods, April/May and July/August. Replacement clutch.
Nestlings blue-grey down; red

inside mouth, yellow gape-flanges. Remain in nest for 12–15 days.

Scarlet Grosbeak *Carpodacus erythrinus*
Pl. **194**

Site thorn bushes and tangled briars, often at height of 1–2 m from the ground, also recorded in trees (oak). Favours dense thick-ets in vicinity of water or on swampy ground. (E. Germany, Finland, Sweden.)
Nest light structure of fine twigs, grass rootlets and lichen with an inner layer of rootlets, fine fibrous material and animal hair. Rem-iniscent of Warbler (*Sylvia*) nest, except for absence of spiders' webs.
Eggs 4–5, less often 6; blue ground colour, marked with a few dark brown, black or dark purple spots and streaks, zoned at the blunt end. Size 20·0 × 14·3 mm. Incubation 12 days (according to Steinfatt-Schwa-nitz). Single brood, June–early July. Replacement clutch.
Nestlings bright red inside mouth; yellow gape-flanges. Remain in nest for 11–13 days (according to Steinfatt-Schwanitz).

Crossbill* *Loxia curvirostra*
Pl. **163**

Site in conifers (spruce, pine), several metres from the ground on a horizontal branch, usually some distance from the trunk. (Scottish race breeds regularly in Highlands, nominate race mainly sporadic breeder in Br. Is.)
Nest solidly built out of twigs,

grass, lichen, moss and bits of bark, lined with wool, finer grass, animal hair and feathers.

Eggs sometimes 3, most commonly 4; drab greenish-white ground colour, marked with reddish-brown, black and purple spots, zoned at the blunt end. Size 22·1 × 16·1 mm. Weight 2·9 g. Incubation 12–13 days. One to two broods, any time of year but mostly February–April.

Nestlings dark grey down; dark red inside mouth, pale pinkish gape-flanges. Remain in nest for 14 days.

Parrot Crossbill *Loxia pytyopsittacus*
Pl. **164**

Site conifer forests, favouring pine but also in spruce, usually high up in trees. (Suspected breeding in Surrey in 1963.)

Nest same type as Crossbill but lined only with fine grass.

Eggs 3–4; similar to Crossbill but slightly larger. Size 23·0 × 16·7 mm. Weight 3·4(?) g. Incubation approx. 13–14 days. One to two broods, any time of year but mostly January–March.

Nestlings remain in nest for about 14 days.

Chaffinch* *Fringilla coelebs*
Pl. **103, 165, 166**

Site bushes, hedges and trees, often in a fork, generally at a height of 2–6 m above the ground.

Nest very neat and compact, woven out of grass, roots and bark fibres, felted with moss and spiders' webs, and decorated with lichen; lined with hair and a few feathers.

Eggs 4–6; ground colour varies from pale blue or blue-grey to greyish-brown and reddish-brown; there are usually a few dark brown spots and blackish scrawls, edged purplish-grey, but occasionally no marking at all. The scrawls look as though they were made with a branding iron. Size 19·3 × 14·6 mm. Weight 2·1 g. Incubation 12–13 days. Two broods, April–June. Replacement clutch.

Nestlings greyish-yellow down; red inside mouth, whitish-yellow gape-flanges. Remain in nest for 13–14 days.

Brambling* *Fringilla montifringilla*
Pl. **102, 167**

Site in trees and bushes at northern latitudes, favouring birch but also in alder, pine and spruce. Nests in small colonies, often at a height of 2–6(8) m from the ground. (Probably breeds sporadically in Scotland.)

Nest same type as Chaffinch but not as neatly constructed; made out of grass, roots, lichen, moss, spiders' webs and bark fibres, lined with hair and small feathers. Decorated effect makes it difficult to spot.

Eggs 5–6; very variable, similar to Chaffinch with typical black scrawls. Size 19·5 × 14·6 mm (according to Rey). Weight 2·2 g. Incubation 12–13, occasionally 14 days. Probably two broods (late May–June/July). Cuckoo-host frequently.

Nestlings remain in nest for about 13–14 days.

BUNTINGS *Emberizidae*

Nests are of simple construction, made out of grass and roots, lined with hair. They are generally on the ground in a small depression, hidden by hummocks or stones, and occasionally at a low height, lodged in vegetation. The ground colour of the eggs is variable: drab white, bluish-white, greyish or pinkish-buff, greenish (Cirl Bunting); yellowish-white (Snow Bunting); olive-brown or reddish-brown (Reed Bunting). Eggs of Buntings are marked with brownish-black spots, grey shell-marks and characteristic scrawls or hair-lines. There are usually 5–6 eggs per clutch and two broods per year (Snow Bunting single-brooded). Six species breed in central Europe, five in Br. Is.; Snow Bunting does not breed in central Europe, Rock and Ortolan Buntings do not breed in Br. Is.

Corn Bunting* *Emberiza calandra*
Pl. **141, 170**

Site in a natural hollow on verges, under grass and thistles on waste ground, in meadows or among clover and cereal crops.
Nest loosely built out of bents and fine roots, lined with animal hair, plant down and fine grasses.
Eggs occasionally 4, generally 5–6; ground colour drab white or grey flushed red, irregularly marked with brownish-black spots, scrawls and hair-lines. Size 23·8 × 17·7 mm. Weight 3·7 g. Incubation 12–13 days. Two broods, late April/May–July/August.
Nestlings long yellowish-brown down; pinkish-red inside mouth, pale yellow gape-flanges. Remain in nest for 9–10, sometimes 11 days.

Yellowhammer* *Emberiza citrinella*
Pl. **142, 169, 254**

Site on the ground in a natural hollow hidden by tall grass or up to 50 cm in a bush or hedge, often on uncultivated verges.

Nest made out of dry grass and fine roots, lined with hair (horse-hair) and finer grasses. Nests in bushes tend to be more substantial than those on the ground.
Eggs 3–5, sometimes 6; very variable ground colour drab white or bluish-white, white flushed red or light reddish-brown, with dark brown spots, hair-lines and grey shell-marks. Size 21·2 × 15·9 mm. Weight 2·7 g. Incubation 12–14 days. Two broods, April–July, occasionally three. Replacement clutch. Cuckoo-host frequently.
Nestlings grey down on head and back; pinkish inside mouth, yellow gape-flanges. Remain in nest for 12–13 days.

Cirl Bunting* *Emberiza cirlus*
Pl. **171**

Site in bushes, hedges and bramble thickets, mostly at knee-height but occasionally at ground level. (Now confined to southern England.)
Nest similar to Yellowhammer, made out of bents, lined with fine grasses and animal hair.
Eggs 3–5, pale green or bluish-

185

white ground colour, marked with brownish-black spots and fine hair-lines. Size 20·9 × 15·9 mm. Weight 2·8 g. Incubation 11–13 days. Two broods, late April–July, sometimes a third brood in Br. Is.

Nestlings long greyish-brown down; pink inside mouth, yellow gape-flanges. Remain in nest for 10–13 days.

Rock Bunting *Emberiza cia*
Pl. **172**

Site in a natural hollow on the ground between stones, under roots or tufts of vegetation; also in low bushes and occasionally in vineyard walls.

Nest similar to Yellowhammer, made out of bents and fine roots, lined with fine grasses and horse-hair.

Eggs 4–6; ground colour greyish-white, bluish or pinkish-buff, marked with isolated spots (dark brown and grey) and fine scrawls (brownish-black). Size 20·6 × 16·0 mm. Weight approx. 2·5 g. Incubation 12–13 days. Two broods, May–June.

Nestlings grey down; reddish inside mouth, yellowish gape-flanges. Remain in nest for 10–13 days.

Ortolan Bunting *Emberiza hortulana*
Pl. **143**

Site in a natural hollow on verges with grass and weeds, also in low bushes on waste ground and in cultivated fields (brassica, corn, potato crops).

Nest similar to Yellowhammer, made out of roots and grass, lined with hair and fine grasses.

Eggs 5, less often 6; ground colour bluish-grey, pinkish-grey, whitish-grey or yellowish-brown, marked with a few brownish-black spots, blotches and hair-lines. Size 19·7 × 15·3 mm. Weight 2·3 g. Incubation 11–13, sometimes 14, days. Two broods, May–June.

Nestlings pale grey down; red inside mouth, yellow gape-flanges. Remain in nest for 10–12, occasionally 13, days.

Snow Bunting* *Plectrophenax nivalis*
Pl. **168**

Site hidden among stones, on high ground with scree or loose boulders. (A few pairs nest regularly in Scotland; main breeding areas are in the far north.)

Nest made of dry grass, lichen and moss; lining often consists of lots of feathers but there may be animal hair or down and fine grass.

Eggs sometimes 4, mostly 5–6; yellowish or greenish-white ground colour, marked with reddish-brown and blackish-brown spots with mauve edges and fine hair-lines. Size 22·4 × 16·8 mm. Weight 1·7 g. Incubation 10–13 days. Single brood, mid-May–June/July.

Nestlings remain in nest for 11–14 days.

Reed Bunting* *Emberiza schoeniclus*
Pl. **144**

Site usually on the ground, sometimes close above it, on a dry spot in a damp habitat; hidden among reeds and rushes near water, between the roots of alder, in nettles or similar rank vegetation in marshy places.

Nest loosely built out of grass and bits of reeds, lined with hair and fine grasses.

Eggs 5–6, sometimes only 4; ground colour olive-brown or reddish-brown, marked with well-defined brownish-black spots and scrawls, and pale grey shell-marks. Size 19·3 × 14·3 mm. Weight 2·1 g. Incubation 13–14 days. Two broods, late April–July.
Nestlings pink skin, grey down on head and back; red inside mouth, pale yellow gape-flanges. Remain in nest for 11–13 days.

SPARROWS   *Ploceidae*

As well as the true Sparrows (*Passer* species), Snow Finch and Rock Sparrow are included in this group. The presence of lots of feathers in the nest is typical. Eggs are densely marked with brownish spots (Snow Finch is uniform white); although the ground colour varies, it is mostly whitish. There are generally 5–6 eggs per clutch and two to three broods per year (Snow Finch is single-brooded). Four species breed in central Europe, two in Br. Is.

House Sparrow* *Passer domesticus*
Pl. **113, 200**
Site in holes and crevices, often on buildings, (under tiles, in drainpipes, etc.), also in trees and nestboxes; other sites include nests of other species, particularly House Martin, or among the outer twigs of large nests (Stork and large Birds of Prey). Nests in open sites such as fruit trees, are domed or fully 'roofed', with entrance-holes at the side towards the top.
Nest untidily built out of straw, rootlets, bits of paper, wool or similar waste material; lining consists of lots of feathers.
Eggs 5–6; variable, white, bluish-white or greenish ground colour, strongly marked with grey to brown spots, zoned at the blunt end. Size 22·5 × 15·7 mm. Weight 3 g. Incubation 13 days. Usually three broods, March/April–August, occasionally four.
Nestlings no down; pale pinkish-blue inside mouth. Remain in nest for 15–16 days.

Tree Sparrow* *Passer montanus*
Pl. **114, 199**
Site holes in trees and walls, under roofs, in nestboxes and also in rock crevices; like House Sparrow, nests are domed when built in comparatively open sites.
Nest similar to House Sparrow, made out of roots, wool fibres, straw, grass, moss, etc., lined with animal hair, grass and lots of feathers. Some nests are decorated with brightly-coloured wool (etc.), others are little more than feathers stuffed in a crevice.

More than one nest is built, some being used only for roosting.

Eggs 5–6, less often 7; whitish with dark spots which vary from grey to deep brown; there is nearly always one egg in the clutch which is paler than the rest. Size 19·3 × 14·0 mm. Weight around 2 g. Incubation 13–14 days. Two broods, April–July, occasionally three. Replacement clutch.

Nestlings pink skin, no down; purple inside mouth. Remain in nest for about 16 days.

Rock Sparrow *Petronia petronia* Pl. **198**

Site deep in rock crevices or in holes of walls and ruins, less frequently holes in trees. Nests may be on their own or in small colonies.

Nest made out of roots, grass and fibrous material, lined with hair, wool and feathers.

Eggs 4–5, sometimes 6; yellowish, dirty white or brownish ground colour, marked with reddish-brown or dark brown spots, thickly zoned at the blunt end (reminiscent of House Sparrow). Size 21·3 × 15·6 mm. Incubation around 14 days. Two broods, May–July.

Nestlings pale grey down on mantle and head; blue-red inside mouth, reddish-yellow gape-flanges. Remain in nest for about 21 days.

Snow Finch *Montifringilla nivalis* (Not illustrated)

Site confined to mountain districts; in rock crevices, among scree and boulders, and occasionally on buildings at high altitudes (holes in walls, under roofs).

Nest bulky, made out of grass and roots, felted with moss and lichen, and lined with feathers, wool and hair.

Eggs 4–5; matt surface, pure white. Size 23·4 × 16·9 mm. Weight approx. 4 g. Incubation about 18 days (according to Makatsch). Single brood, May–July, possibly two broods.

Nestlings long white down; yellow gape-flanges. Remain in nest for about 17 days.

SELECTED BIBLIOGRAPHY

Campbell, B, and Ferguson-Lees, J *A Field Guide to Birds' Nests* Constable 1972

Landsborough Thomson, A *A New Dictionary of Birds* Nelson 1970

Mayer-Gross, H *The Nest Record Scheme* (B.T.O. Field Guide No. 12) 1970

Peterson, R. T, Mountfort, G, and Hollom, P. A. D *A Field Guide to the Birds of Britain and Europe* Collins 1966

Reade, W, and Hosking, E *Nesting Birds, Eggs and Fledglings* Blandford 1974

Voous, K. H *Atlas of European Birds* Nelson 1960

Witherby, H. F, Jourdain, F. C. R, Ticehurst, N. F, and Tucker, B. W *The Handbook of British Birds* Witherby 1943

ACKNOWLEDGEMENTS

The author and publisher wish to thank the following for help with the preparation of the text and illustrations: Frau Christa Reinwarth, Frau Dr Katharina Heinroth, Dr Wolfgang Makatsch, Dr Heinz Lehmann and Herr Horst Hethke.

Aichhorn, Prof. Ambros, **Pl nos.** 111, 126; Ausobsky, Albert, 52, 123; Christiansen, Arthur, 12, 13, 14, 19, 34, 51, 60, 65, 99, 102; Hable, Dr Erich, 35; Hosking, Eric, 1, 6, 48, 131, 133, 138; Kuch, Erich, 130; Limbrunner, Alfred, 57; Löhrl, Dr Hans, 119; Quedens, Georg, 3, 4, 5, 7, 9, 10, 11, 18, 20, 21, 22, 31, 32, 33, 37, 39, 42, 43, 44, 45, 47, 50, 54, 59, 87, 127, 129, 132, 136, 137; Reinwarth, Christa, 8, 15, 16, 24, 25, 26, 27, 28, 29, 36, 38, 41, 49, 53, 55, 56, 62, 63, 66, 67, 68, 69, 70, 71, 72, 75, 76, 78, 79, 80, 81, 83, 84, 86, 88, 91, 94, 95, 96, 103, 104, 105, 106, 107, 108, 109, 113, 114, 121, 122, 124, 125, 136, 139, 140, 142, 144; Schrempp, Heinz, 17, 30, 46, 61, 64, 73, 74, 77, 82, 85, 89, 92, 93, 97, 98, 100, 101, 110, 112, 118, 134, 135, 141, 251, 252, 253, 254, 255, 256; Schwammberger, Karl, 40, 115, 116, 117, 120, 128, 143 and Zingel, Dieter, 2, 19, 23, 58.

INDEX OF ENGLISH NAMES

Numbers in **bold** refer to the plates.

INDEX OF LATIN NAMES